Networking and Information Technology Research and Development
National Coordination Office

I0002756

Keith A. Marzullo
Director

Peter Lyster
Deputy Director

Margaret E. Harmsen
Editor

Diane R. Theiss
Budget Analyst

4201 Wilson Boulevard, Suite II-405
Arlington, Virginia 22230
(703) 292-4873
nco@nitrd.gov

Acknowledgments
This Supplement to the President's Budget was developed through the contributions of the NITRD Federal agency representatives and members, the NCO staff, and other Federal agencies participating in the NITRD Program. We extend our sincere thanks and appreciation to all who have contributed.

National Coordination Office for Networking and Information Technology Research and Development
The annual NITRD Supplement to the President's Budget is prepared and published by the National Coordination Office for Networking and Information Technology Research and Development (NITRD/NCO). The NCO staff coordinates the activities of the NITRD Program and supports overall planning, budget, and assessment activities for the multiagency NITRD enterprise under the auspices of the NITRD Subcommittee of the National Science and Technology Council's (NSTC) Committee on Technology (CoT).

About the Document
This document is a supplement to the President's Fiscal Year 2017 Budget Request. It describes the activities underway in 2016 and planned for 2017 by the Federal agencies participating in the NITRD Program, primarily from a programmatic and budgetary perspective. It reports actual investments for FY 2015, estimated investments for FY 2016, and requested funding levels for FY 2017 by Program Component Area (PCA). It identifies the NITRD Program's strategic priorities by PCA for budgetary requests; strategic priorities underlying the requests; highlights of the requests; planning and coordination activities supporting the request; and 2016 and 2017 activities by agency.

SUPPLEMENT TO THE PRESIDENT'S BUDGET
FOR FISCAL YEAR 2017

THE NETWORKING AND INFORMATION TECHNOLOGY RESEARCH AND DEVELOPMENT PROGRAM

A Report by the
Subcommittee on Networking and Information Technology
Research and Development

Committee on Technology
National Science and Technology Council

APRIL 2016

National Science and Technology Council Committee on Technology
Thomas Kalil, Chair, OSTP
Afua Bruce, Executive Secretary, OSTP

Subcommittee on Networking and Information Technology Research and Development
Co-Chairs
James F. Kurose, NSF, and Keith A. Marzullo, NCO

Department of Commerce

NIST
Representative
Charles H. Romine
Alternate
Kamie Roberts

NOAA
Representative
Brian Gross

Department of Defense

DARPA
Representative
John Launchbury

NSA
Representative
Christopher D. Green
Alternate
Candace S. Culhane

OSD
Representative
Richard Linderman
Alternate
Dai H. Kim

SERVICE RESEARCH ORGANIZATIONS:
Air Force
Representative
Anthony M. Newton

Army
Representative
Mary J. Miller
Alternate
Karen L. O'Conner

Navy
Representative
Sukarno Mertoguno

Department of Energy

DOE/NNSA
Representative
Douglas Wade
Alternate
Thuc T. Hoang

DOE/OE
Representative
Carol Hawk

DOE/SC
Representative
J. Steve Binkley
Alternates
William Harrod
Barbara Helland

Department of Health and Human Services

AHRQ
Representative
Edwin A. Lomotan
Alternate
Tiffani Bright

NIH
Representative
Susan Gregurick
Alternate
Vinay M. Pai

ONC
Representative
Jamie Skipper

Department of Homeland Security

DHS
Representative
Douglas Maughan
Alternate
Luke Berndt

Department of Justice

NIJ
Representative
William Ford
Alternate
Mark Greene

EPA
Representative
Gary L. Walter

NASA
Representative
Bryan A. Biegel

NARA
Representative
Mark Conrad

NRO
Representative
Robert Jimenez
Alternate
Richard D. Ridgley

NSF
Representative
James F. Kurose
Alternate
Erwin Gianchandani

OMB
Representative
Tali Bar-Shalom

OSTP
Representative
Afua Bruce

NITRD/NCO
Representative
Keith A. Marzullo
Alternate
Peter Lyster
Executive Secretary
Nekeia Butler

April 21, 2016

Members of Congress:

I am pleased to transmit the Networking and Information Technology Research and Development (NITRD) Program's FY 2017 Annual Supplement to the President's Budget. The NITRD Program, which today comprises 21 member agencies and many additional participating agencies, coordinates Federal research and development (R&D) investments in advanced digital technologies that are essential for the Nation's economy, security, and quality of life. NITRD agencies collaborate closely in the planning and execution of their respective research programs, leveraging Federal investments in a highly coordinated manner. These efforts enable the Program as a whole to have a more far-reaching and greater positive impact than the agencies could achieve working alone. I note that, with this Budget Supplement, the NITRD Program is modernizing its budget reporting categories (Program Component Areas) to reflect evolving IT R&D priorities and focus areas that are important for the Program's future direction.

Networking and information technologies have transformed the lives of all Americans and revolutionized capabilities across the globe for commerce, government, science, and education. Advances in digital technologies continue to be crucial to the Nation's economic growth, innovation, and job creation, and are essential to continued progress in developing new capabilities in domains such as the sciences, national security, manufacturing, health, energy, education, transportation, and the environment.

President Obama has emphasized that networking and computing capabilities will also provide critical foundations for a number of key priorities, including expanding the frontiers of knowledge about the human brain; employing genetics to develop cures and treatments tailored to individuals; developing sustainable energy sources and energy delivery systems; improving climate models; and ensuring an open and free Internet that is secure, resilient, and affords appropriate privacy protections. In addition, a new national computing initiative will bring coherence and alignment in technology research to produce not only a more powerful computing platform but also provide the launching pad for the United States to lead the next evolution in computing beyond Moore's Law, fostering U.S. competitiveness and ensuring the Nation's science and technology leadership.

Federal NITRD investments made today are crucial to the creation of tomorrow's new industries and workforce opportunities. I look forward to continuing to work with you to support this vital Federal program.

Sincerely,

John P. Holdren
Assistant to the President for Science and Technology
Director, Office of Science and Technology Policy

Contents

NITRD Member Agencies

The following Federal agencies conduct or support R&D in advanced networking and information technologies, report their IT research budgets in the NITRD crosscut, and provide support for program coordination:

Department of Commerce (DOC)
    National Institute of Standards and Technology (NIST)
    National Oceanic and Atmospheric Administration (NOAA)
Department of Defense (DoD)
    Defense Advanced Research Projects Agency (DARPA)
    National Security Agency (NSA)
    Office of the Secretary of Defense (OSD)
    Service Research Organizations (Air Force, Army, Navy)
Department of Energy (DOE)
    National Nuclear Security Administration (DOE/NNSA)
    Office of Electricity Delivery and Energy Reliability (DOE/OE)
    Office of Science (DOE/SC)
Department of Health and Human Services (HHS)
    Agency for Healthcare Research and Quality (AHRQ)
    National Institutes of Health (NIH)
    Office of the National Coordinator for Health Information Technology (ONC)
Department of Homeland Security (DHS)
    Science and Technology Directorate (S&T)
Department of Justice (DOJ)
    National Institute of Justice (NIJ)
Environmental Protection Agency (EPA)
National Aeronautics and Space Administration (NASA)
National Archives and Records Administration (NARA)
National Reconnaissance Office (NRO)
National Science Foundation (NSF)

NITRD Participating Agencies

The following Federal agencies participate in NITRD activities and have mission interests that involve applications and R&D in advanced networking and information technologies:

Department of Commerce (DOC)
    National Telecommunications and Information Administration (NTIA)
Department of Defense (DoD)
    Defense Health Agency (DHA)
    Department of Defense Intelligence Information Systems (DoDIIS)
    Joint Improvised Explosive Device Defeat Organization (JIEDDO)
    National Computer Security Center (NCSC)
    National Geospatial-Intelligence Agency (NGA)
    Telemedicine and Advanced Technology Research Center (TATRC)
Department of Education (ED)
Department of Energy (DOE)
    Office of Environmental Management (DOE/EM)
Department of Health and Human Services (HHS)
    Centers for Disease Control and Prevention (CDC)
    Food and Drug Administration (FDA)
Department of Homeland Security (DHS)
    Customs and Border Protection (CBP)
    Federal Protective Service (FPS)
    Transportation Security Administration (TSA)
Department of Interior (Interior)
    National Park Service (NPS)
    U.S. Geological Survey (USGS)
Department of Justice (DOJ)
    Federal Bureau of Investigation (FBI)
Department of Labor (DOL)
    Bureau of Labor Statistics (BLS)
Department of State (State)
Department of Transportation (DOT)
    Federal Aviation Administration (FAA)
    Federal Highway Administration (FHWA)
Department of the Treasury (Treasury)
    Office of Financial Research (OFR)
Department of Veterans Affairs (VA)
Federal Communications Commission (FCC)
Federal Deposit Insurance Corporation (FDIC)
General Services Administration (GSA)
Nuclear Regulatory Commission (NRC)
Office of the Director of National Intelligence (ODNI)
    Intelligence Advanced Research Projects Activity (IARPA)
    National Counterterrorism Center (NCTC)
U.S. Agency for International Development (USAID)
U.S. Department of Agriculture (USDA)
    Agricultural Research Service (ARS)
    National Institute of Food and Agriculture (NIFA)

Introduction and Overview

The Networking and Information Technology Research and Development (NITRD) Program is the Nation's primary source of federally funded work on advanced information technologies (IT) in computing, networking, and software. The multiagency NITRD Program seeks to provide the research and development (R&D) foundations for assuring continued U.S. technological leadership and meeting the needs of the Federal Government for advanced information technologies. The NITRD Program also seeks to accelerate development and deployment of advanced information technologies in order to maintain world leadership in science and engineering, enhance national defense and national and homeland security, improve U.S. productivity and economic competitiveness, protect the environment, and improve the health, education, and quality of life of all Americans.

Now in its 25th year, the NITRD Program is one of the oldest and largest of the formal Federal programs that engage multiple agencies in coordination activities. As required by the High-Performance Computing Act of 1991 (P.L. 102-194), the Next Generation Internet Research Act of 1998 (P.L. 105-305), and the America COMPETES (Creating Opportunities to Meaningfully Promote Excellence in Technology, Education, and Science) Act of 2007 (P.L. 110-69), the NITRD Program provides a framework and mechanisms for coordination among the Federal agencies that support advanced IT R&D and report IT research budgets in the NITRD crosscut. Many other agencies with IT interests also participate in NITRD activities.

Highlights of the NITRD Program over the past year include:

- *Review of the NITRD Program*: In August 2015, the President's Council of Advisors on Science and Technology (PCAST) released the *Report to the President and Congress Ensuring Leadership in Federally Funded Research and Development in Information Technology.*[1] The report provides the PCAST's findings from its biennial review of the NITRD Program and recommendations on modernizing the Program's R&D investment portfolio and coordination process. Activities are currently underway in response to the PCAST's recommendations on NITRD coordination.

- *Changes to Program Component Areas*: Beginning with the FY 2017 budget cycle, the NITRD Program is transitioning its eight Program Component Areas (PCAs) to a new set of 10 PCAs. These changes reflect the IT R&D priorities and focus areas on which the NITRD Program's future direction is being set. Implementing these changes necessitates updates in NITRD budget reporting in order to track and measure PCA funding levels. The PCA changes are detailed in the next section of this document.

- *Cybersecurity R&D Strategy*: With leadership from the Office of Science and Technology Policy (OSTP), NITRD agencies completed the *Federal Cybersecurity Research and Development Strategic Plan: Ensuring Prosperity and National Security.*[2] The Plan was released by the NSTC and delivered to Congress as mandated by the Cybersecurity Enhancement Act of 2014 (P.L. 113-274).

- *National Strategic Computing Initiative*: In July 2015, the President issued Executive Order 13702 to create the National Strategic Computing Initiative (NSCI).[3] The 2017 Budget supports NSCI investments through many agencies, with major investments from the Department of Energy (DOE) and the National Science Foundation (NSF). NITRD agencies will continue to coordinate their high-end computing research activities

---

[1] *Report to the President and Congress Ensuring Leadership in Federally Funded Research and Development in Information Technology*. August 2015, President's Council of Advisors on Science and Technology:
https://www.whitehouse.gov/sites/default/files/microsites/ostp/PCAST/nitrd_report_aug_2015.pdf.
[2] *Federal Cybersecurity Research and Development Strategic Plan: Ensuring Prosperity and National Security*. February 2016, NSTC:
https://www.whitehouse.gov/sites/whitehouse.gov/files/documents/2016_Federal_Cybersecurity_Research_and_Development_Stratgeic_Plan.pdf.
[3] Executive Order 13702 (EO 13702): Creating a National Strategic Computing Initiative. July 29, 2015:
https://www.federalregister.gov/articles/2015/08/03/2015-19183/creating-a-national-strategic-computing-initiative.

through the High End Computing Interagency Working Group (HEC IWG), while aligning with the national-level computing strategy of the NSCI.

- **Big Data R&D Strategy**: The Big Data Senior Steering Group (BD SSG) is completing *The Federal Big Data Research and Development Strategic Plan*, which is expected to be released in 2016.

- **Privacy R&D Strategy**: In 2014 OSTP tasked the NITRD Cybersecurity R&D SSG to define a privacy research framework by soliciting broad inputs from academia, government, and industry and, building on those inputs, to develop a draft National Privacy Research Strategy. The strategy is expected to be released in 2016.

- **NITRD Membership**: This past year, the NITRD Program welcomed the Department of Justice's National Institute of Justice (NIJ) as a new member.

Changes to the NITRD Budget Reporting Structure

The 2015 PCAST review of the NITRD Program included a recommendation to revise the NITRD R&D investment portfolio to reflect both the current nature of IT and the national priorities in which IT plays a major role. Based on an internal review, the NITRD/NCO recommended modernizing the NITRD Program's budget categories. Beginning with the FY 2017 budget request, and with concurrence from the NITRD Subcommittee and Executive Branch stakeholders, the NITRD Program is changing its budget reporting structure.

The NITRD budget reporting structure is comprised of Program Component Areas (PCAs), which are the major subject areas under which the projects and activities coordinated through the NITRD Program are grouped. As required by law, NITRD agencies report their levels of Federal funding in the PCAs in the annual NITRD budget crosscut. Effective with the FY 2017 budget, the number of PCAs will increase from eight to 10. Of the 10 PCAs, four will be new, three will be impacted by the newly defined PCAs, and three will remain unchanged. The changes are highlighted in the PCA definitions provided further along in this section.

Below is a summary view of the NITRD PCAs used prior to FY 2017 and of the new set of PCAs for FY 2017.

Pre-FY 2017 PCAs
• Cybersecurity and Information Assurance (CSIA)
• High Confidence Software and Systems (HCSS)
• High End Computing Infrastructure and Applications (HEC I&A)
• High End Computing Research and Development (HEC R&D)
• Human Computer Interaction and Information Management (HCI&IM)
• Large Scale Networking (LSN)
• Social, Economic, and Workforce Implications of IT and IT Workforce Development (SEW)
• Software Design and Productivity (SDP)
FY 2017 PCAs
• [NEW] Enabling-R&D for High-Capability Computing Systems (EHCS)
• [NEW] High-Capability Computing Systems Infrastructure and Applications (HCSIA)
• [NEW] Large-Scale Data Management and Analysis (LSDMA)
• [NEW] Robotics and Intelligent Systems (RIS)
• [IMPACTED] Human Computer Interaction and Information Management (HCI&IM)
• [IMPACTED] High Confidence Software and Systems (HCSS)
• [IMPACTED] Large Scale Networking (LSN)
• [UNCHANGED] Cyber Security and Information Assurance (CSIA)
• [UNCHANGED] Social, Economic, and Workforce Implications of IT and IT Workforce Development (SEW)
• [UNCHANGED] Software Design and Productivity (SDP)

The following diagram illustrates the relationship between the PCAs used prior to FY 2017 and the FY 2017 PCAs.

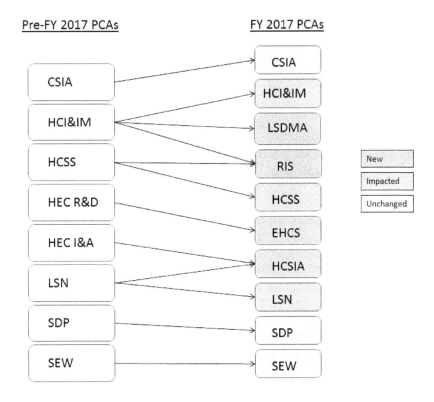

The definitions for the new set of PCAs for FY 2017 are provided below and include a characterization of the budget reporting status and impact of this year's changes on each PCA.

FY 2017 NITRD Program Component Area Definitions

Acronym	Name	Definition
CSIA	Cyber Security and Information Assurance	[UNCHANGED] CSIA focuses on research and development to detect, prevent, resist, respond to, and recover from actions that compromise or threaten to compromise the availability, integrity, or confidentiality of computer- and network-based systems. These systems provide the IT foundation in every sector of the economy, including critical infrastructures such as power grids, financial systems, and air-traffic-control networks. These systems also support national defense, homeland security, and other Federal missions. Broad areas of emphasis include Internet and network security; security of information and computer-based systems; approaches to achieving hardware and software security; testing and assessment of computer-based systems security; reconstitution of computer-based systems and data; and resilience against cyber-attacks on computer-based systems that monitor, protect, and control critical infrastructure.
EHCS	Enabling-R&D for High-Capability Computing Systems	[NEW] Research and development to enable advancements in high-capability computing systems, spanning the hardware, software, architecture, system performance, computational algorithms, data analytics, development tools, and software methods for extreme data- and compute-intensive workloads; and developing fundamentally new approaches to high-capability computing systems.

Acronym	Name	Definition
HCSIA	High-Capability Computing Systems Infrastructure and Applications	[NEW] High-capability computing systems (HCS) and associated application software, communications, storage, data management, and HCS infrastructure to meet agency mission needs.
HCSS	High Confidence Software and Systems	[IMPACTED] HCSS R&D supports development of scientific foundations and innovative and enabling software and hardware technologies for the engineering, verification and validation, assurance, standardization, and certification of complex, networked, distributed computing systems and cyber-physical (IT-enabled) systems (CPS). The goal is to enable seamless, fully synergistic integration of computational intelligence, communication, control, sensing, actuation, and adaptation with physical devices and information processes to routinely realize high-confidence, optimally performing systems that are essential for effectively operating life-, safety-, security-, and mission-critical applications. These systems must be capable of interacting correctly, safely, and securely with humans and the physical world in changing environments and unforeseen conditions. In many cases, they must be certifiably dependable. The vision is to realize dependable systems that are precise and highly efficient; respond quickly; work in dangerous or inaccessible environments; provide large-scale, distributed coordination; augment human capabilities; and enhance societal quality of life. New science and technology are needed to build these systems with computing, communication, information, and control pervasively embedded at all levels, thus enabling entirely new generations of engineering designs that can enhance U.S. competitiveness across economic and industrial sectors. *Impact of RIS on HCSS budget reporting:* • *Budget for the portion of HCSS that covered robotics will be reported under RIS.*
HCI&IM	Human Computer Interaction and Information Management	[IMPACTED] Human computer interaction, collaboration, and communication technologies and information management to expand human capabilities, enabled through research on visualization, collaborative systems, multimodal system engagements, and advancements in understanding human cognition, including perception, intuition, learning, cognitive load, and problem solving for human-in-the-loop systems. *Impact of LSDMA and RIS on HCI&IM budget reporting:* • *Budget for the portion of HCI&IM that covered big data, large-scale data analytics, and information management will be reported under LSDMA.* • *Budget for the portion of HCI&IM that covered robotics will be reported under RIS.*
LSDMA	Large-Scale Data Management and Analysis	[NEW] Large-scale data management and analysis to develop the ability to analyze and extract knowledge and insight from large, diverse, and disparate sources of data, including structures for data capture, curation, management, and access.

Acronym	Name	Definition
LSN	Large Scale Networking	[IMPACTED] LSN focuses on coordinating Federal agency networking R&D in leading-edge networking technologies, services, and enhanced performance. This includes programs in fundamental networking research and architectures, future Internet architectures, wireless networks, software-defined networks, heterogeneous multimedia networks, testbeds, and end-to-end performance and performance measurement. Program coordination also spans network security, privacy, and identity management; dynamic inter-domain networking; public service networks; the science and engineering of complex networks; network infrastructures for advanced discovery environments; network-enabling technology; networking education, training, and outreach; and cyberinfrastructure for scientific and applications R&D. *Impact of HCSIA on LSN budget reporting:* • *Budget for the portion of LSN that covers large-scale networking infrastructure in support of high-capability computing will be reported under HCSIA.*
RIS	Robotics and Intelligent Systems	[NEW] Robotics and intelligent systems to advance physical and computational agents that complement, augment, enhance, or emulate human physical capabilities or human intelligence. This includes robotics hardware and software design, application, and practical use; machine perception; intelligent cognition, adaptation, and learning; mobility and manipulation; human-robot interaction; distributed and networked robotics; increasingly autonomous systems; and related applications.
SDP	Software Design and Productivity	[UNCHANGED] The SDP R&D agenda spans the science and the technology of software creation and sustainment (e.g., development methods and environments, Verification and Validation (V&V) technologies, component technologies, languages, and tools) and software project management in diverse domains. R&D will advance software engineering concepts, methods, techniques, and tools that result in more usable, dependable, cost-effective, evolvable, and sustainable software-intensive systems. The domains cut across information technology, industrial production, evolving areas such as the Internet, and highly complex, interconnected software-intensive systems. The core SDP R&D activities are software productivity, software cost, responsiveness to change, and sustainment. The success of these activities can have a major beneficial effect on high-confidence systems because such systems are critically dependent upon the quality of the software and on the many companies producing software-reliant products.
SEW	Social, Economic, and Workforce Implications of IT and IT Workforce Development	[UNCHANGED] Research activities funded under the SEW PCA focus on the co-evolution of IT and social, economic, and workforce systems, including interactions between people and IT and among people developing and using IT in groups, organizations, and larger social networks. Collaborative science concerns are addressed including understanding and improving the effectiveness of teams and enhancing geographically distributed, interdisciplinary R&D to engage societal concerns, such as competitiveness, security, economic development, and wellbeing. Workforce concerns are addressed by leveraging interagency efforts to improve education outcomes through the use of learning technologies that anticipate the educational needs of individuals and society. SEW also supports efforts to speed the transfer of R&D results to the policymaker, practitioner, and IT user communities in all sectors.

About the NITRD Supplement to the President's Budget

The annual Supplement to the President's Budget for the NITRD Program provides a technical summary of the research activities planned and coordinated through NITRD in a given Federal budget cycle, as required by law. The details are organized by PCA and presented using a common format:

- Listing of the NITRD member agencies requesting budget in the PCA and other participating agencies active in the PCA

- Definition of the research covered in the PCA

- Strategic priorities in the PCA for the forthcoming fiscal year

- Budget highlights – agencies' key R&D programs and topical emphases in the PCA for the forthcoming year

- Interagency coordination – current and planned activities in which multiple agencies are collaborating

- Ongoing core activities of each agency in the PCA

The NITRD Supplement includes annual budget tables and a budget analysis section, organized by PCA and by agency, to facilitate budgetary and programmatic comparisons from year to year. The budget tables report actual expenditures for FY 2015, estimated expenditures for FY 2016, and proposed funding levels for FY 2017. Note that with the exception of the three PCAs that were not impacted by the new PCAs, and whose definitions did not change—CSIA, SDP, and SEW—the continuity between the PCAs in the pre-FY 2017 set and those in the new FY 2017 set is limited. This affects tracking budget trends over time. Additionally, for purposes of the NITRD budget crosscut, agencies categorized past expenditures for FY 2015 retrospectively because the new set of PCAs did not exist in the FY 2015 timeframe. Any longitudinal comparisons of PCA budgets should take these factors into consideration.

In addition to budget reporting, the Supplement also provides an overview of NITRD Program coordination, a listing of the NITRD Working Groups, and brief descriptions of additional program focus areas.

The President's FY 2017 budget request for the NITRD Program is $4.54 billion and the 2016 NITRD budget estimates totaled $4.49 billion. Details of the budget are presented in the tables on pages 10-11 and discussed in the budget analysis section.

The following illustration shows the percentages of the FY 2017 budget requests by PCA.

FY 2017 Budget Requests by PCA

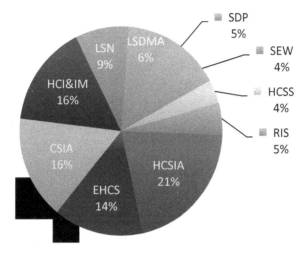

The following illustration shows the percentages of the FY 2017 budget requests by agency.

FY 2017 Budget Requests by Agency

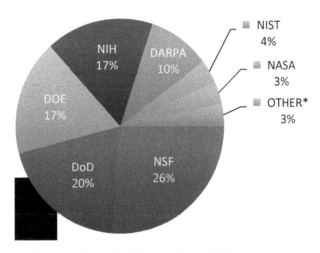

*Includes AHRQ, DHS, EPA, NARA, NIJ, and NOAA.

The following illustration shows budget trends by PCA since FY 2000.[4]

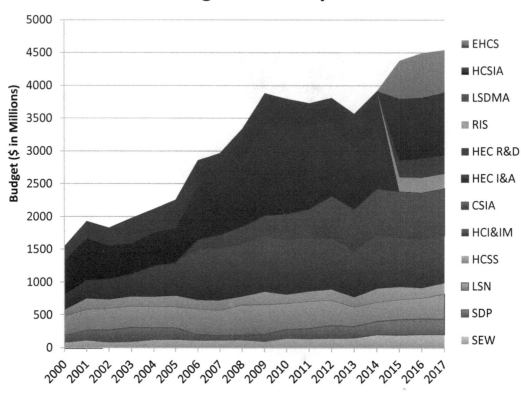

Budget Trends by PCA

Key

EHCS	Enabling-R&D for High-Capability Computing Systems
HCSIA	High-Capability Computing Systems Infrastructure and Applications
LSDMA	Large-Scale Data Management and Analysis
RIS	Robotics and Intelligent Systems
HEC R&D	High End Computing Research and Development
HEC I&A	High End Computing Infrastructure and Applications
CSIA	Cyber Security and Information Assurance
HCI&IM	Human Computer Interaction and Information Management
HCSS	High Confidence Software and Systems
LSN	Large Scale Networking
SDP	Software Design and Productivity
SEW	Social, Economic, and Workforce Implications of IT and IT Workforce Development

Note that budget reporting for CSIA began in FY 2006 and for EHCS, HCSIA, LSDMA, and RIS in FY 2015. Budget reporting for HEC R&D and HEC I&A ended in FY 2014.

---

[4] The budget trends by PCA illustration uses the budget actuals, estimates, and requests provided in the tables on pages 10-11. Budget actuals are used prior to FY 2015, when available; otherwise, estimates are used.

The following illustration shows budget trends by agency since FY 2000.[5]

Budget Trends by Agency

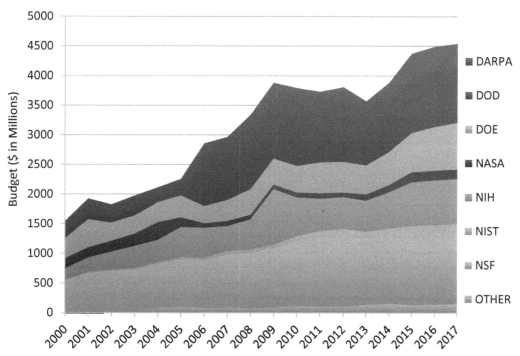

DOD includes OSD and DoD Service research organizations. DOE includes DOE/NNSA, DOE/OE, and DOE/SC. OTHER includes AHRQ, DHS, EPA, NARA, NIJ, and NOAA.

---

[5] The budget trends by agency illustration uses the budget actuals, estimates, and requests provided in the tables on pages 10-11. Budget actuals are used prior to FY 2015, when available; otherwise, estimates are used.

Agency NITRD Budgets by Program Component Area

FY 2015 Budget Actuals (Dollars in Millions)

Agency/ Program Component Area [e]	Cyber Security & Information Assurance	Enabling-R&D for High-Capability Computing Systems	Human Computer Interaction & Information Management	High-Capability Computing Systems Infrastructure & Applications	High Confidence Software & Systems	Large-Scale Data Management & Analysis	Large Scale Networking	Robotics & Intelligent Systems	Software Design & Productivity	Social, Economic, & Workforce Implications of IT	Total [a]
	CSIA	EHCS	HCI&IM	HCSIA	HCSS	LSDMA	LSN	RIS	SDP	SEW	
NSF	107.3	133.1	187.5	189.0	83.7	110.7	134.8	43.1	89.1	127.1	1,205.3
DoD [b]	159.8	251.7	199.2	80.8	28.4	31.9	85.3	96.6	8.9	0.3	942.9
DOE [c]	32.7	123.1		378.8	30.6	7.4	69.3			3.0	644.9
NIH [d]	3.0	23.1	299.0	194.6	29.0		8.0		122.0	51.0	729.7
DARPA	285.5	25.1				85.2					395.8
NIST	65.2	4.4	7.2	8.1	14.7	15.8	9.1	7.9	1.8	4.0	138.3
NASA		1.0	13.0	67.3	8.3	5.0	0.6	63.8	8.6		167.5
DHS	60.6		3.7								64.3
NOAA			0.2	23.0			3.3		3.7		30.2
NNSA		16.7								4.2	20.9
AHRQ			28.2								28.2
EPA		3.2	2.7								5.9
NIJ	0.5		0.5			0.7		0.2		2.8	4.7
NARA			0.2								0.2
Total [a, d]	714.5	581.3	741.4	941.6	194.6	256.7	310.3	211.6	234.1	192.4	4,378.6

FY 2016 Budget Estimates (Dollars in Millions)

Agency/ Program Component Area	Cyber Security & Information Assurance	Enabling-R&D for High-Capability Computing Systems	Human Computer Interaction & Information Management	High-Capability Computing Systems Infrastructure & Applications	High Confidence Software & Systems	Large-Scale Data Management & Analysis	Large Scale Networking	Robotics & Intelligent Systems	Software Design & Productivity	Social, Economic, & Workforce Implications of IT	Total [a]
	CSIA	EHCS	HCI&IM	HCSIA	HCSS	LSDMA	LSN	RIS	SDP	SEW	
NSF	110.5	129.8	187.4	180.4	85.8	110.4	137.8	43.0	84.6	126.2	1,195.9
DoD [b]	146.5	264.6	182.7	80.8	13.3	36.2	84.6	101.8	9.5	3.2	923.1
DOE [c]	30.0	204.3		374.4	2.7	5.9	78.2	15.0		10.0	720.5
NIH [d]	3.0	23.1	313.0	194.6	30.0		8.0		129.0	54.0	754.7
DARPA	292.3	23.8				109.4					425.5
NIST	70.2	4.4	8.2	8.1	15.7	15.8	10.8	7.9	1.8	4.0	146.9
NASA		8.5	14.0	62.8	7.5	5.4	0.7	56.3	6.6		161.9
DHS	63.9		4.0			4.0					71.9
NOAA			0.2	29.7			3.3		3.7		36.9
NNSA		18.7								3.5	22.2
AHRQ			21.5								21.5
EPA		3.5	3.0								6.5
NIJ	1.5					2.5		1.0		0.5	5.5
NARA			0.2								0.2
Total [a, d]	718.0	680.7	734.2	930.8	155.0	289.6	323.4	225.0	235.2	201.4	4,493.3

FY 2017 Budget Requests (Dollars in Millions)

Agency/ Program Component Area	Cyber Security & Information Assurance	Enabling-R&D for High-Capability Computing Systems	Human Computer Interaction & Information Management	High-Capability Computing Systems Infrastructure & Applications	High Confidence Software & Systems	Large-Scale Data Management & Analysis	Large Scale Networking	Robotics & Intelligent Systems	Software Design & Productivity	Social, Economic, & Workforce Implications of IT	Total [a]
	CSIA	EHCS	HCI&IM	HCSIA	HCSS	LSDMA	LSN	RIS	SDP	SEW	Total [a]
NSF	111.0	131.0	182.8	183.2	86.5	111.3	139.0	43.5	82.7	127.1	1,198.0
DoD [b]	145.1	216.4	170.0	81.9	12.9	38.2	108.0	102.9	10.2	3.1	888.7
DOE [c]	30.0	208.3		393.6	17.5		88.0	11.7		10.0	759.1
NIH [d]	3.0	23.1	313.0	194.6	30.0		8.0		129.0	54.0	754.7
DARPA	300.1	6.0				106.6	27.6				440.4
NIST	70.2	18.0	8.2	8.1	15.7	15.8	10.8	7.9	1.8	4.0	160.5
NASA		11.0	14.0	60.9	4.9	5.4	0.8	53.5	6.6		157.0
DHS	66.8		2.0			5.0					73.8
NOAA			0.2	36.0			3.3		3.7		43.2
NNSA		30.0								3.5	33.5
AHRQ			22.9								22.9
EPA		3.7	3.1								6.8
NIJ	1.5						1.0	1.0			3.5
NARA			0.2								0.2
Total [a, d]	727.7	647.5	716.4	958.3	167.5	282.3	386.4	220.5	234.0	201.7	4,542.4

Notes

a) Totals may not sum correctly due to rounding.

b) DoD budget includes funding for OSD and the DoD Service research organizations. DoD Service research organizations include: Air Force Research Laboratory (AFRL), including the Air Force Office of Scientific Research (AFOSR); Army Research Laboratory (ARL), including the Army Research Office (ARO); Naval Research Laboratory (NRL); and Office of Naval Research (ONR). The Communications-Electronics Research, Development, and Engineering Center (CERDEC), Defense Research and Engineering Network (DREN), and High Performance Computing Modernization Program (HPCMP) are under Army. Although DARPA and OSD research organizations are under DoD, they are independent of the research organizations of the DoD Services (Air Force, Army, and Navy). NSA is a research organization under DoD, but does not report NITRD funding.

c) DOE budget includes funding from DOE's Office of Science (SC), Office of Electricity Delivery and Energy Reliability (OE), Advanced Research Projects Agency - Energy (ARPA-E), and the Office of Environmental Management (EM).

d) NIH investments in LSDMA and RIS were not available at the time this Supplement was released. NIH anticipates reporting on these new PCAs in the next NITRD Budget Supplement.

e) Actual expenditures for FY 2015 were categorized into the PCAs retrospectively because the set of PCAs for the FY 2017 request did not exist in the FY 2015 timeframe.

National Strategic Computing Initiative

The 2017 Budget supports NSCI investments through many agencies, with major investments within DOE ($285 million) and NSF ($33 million).

NITRD Program Budget Analysis

Changes to Budget Categories for 2015-2017 NITRD Investments

NITRD investments for 2015 through 2017 are reported here for the first time under the updated PCA categories described in "Changes to the NITRD Budget Reporting Structure" on p. 2. The reporting reflects the first-time use and adoption of the revised PCA categories by NITRD agencies. Note that the revised PCA categories represent an update of how NITRD investments by the Federal Government are tabulated, but not a change in the overall scope. Investments under these revised categories should not be compared directly to investments in the PCAs reported in previous NITRD Budget Supplement reports, with the exception of CSIA, SDP, and SEW, which remain unchanged between the old and new PCA categories.

Fiscal Year Overview for 2016-2017

In the following analysis of the NITRD Program, the President's FY 2017 request is compared with the FY 2016 estimates. Changes in NITRD Program budgets reported in the budget analysis reflect revisions to program budgets due to evolving priorities, as well as Congressional actions and appropriations.

Summary

The President's 2017 budget request for the NITRD Program is $4.54 billion, an increase of $0.05 billion or approximately 1.11 percent, compared to the $4.49 billion 2016 estimate. The overall change is due to both increases and decreases in individual agency NITRD budgets, which are described below.

NITRD Program Budget Analysis by Agency

This section describes changes greater than $10 million between 2016 estimated spending and 2017 requests. Smaller changes are discussed only if they represent shifts in funding focus. Budget numbers in these descriptions are rounded from initial agency numbers with three decimals to the nearest tenth.

DoD

Comparison of 2016 estimate ($923.1 million) and 2017 request ($888.7 million): The decrease of $34.4 million is primarily due to a decrease of $48.2 million in EHCS and a decrease of $12.7 million in HCI&IM, with smaller increases and decreases in other PCAs, partially offset by an increase of $23.4 million in LSN.

DOE

Comparison of 2016 estimate ($720.5 million) and 2017 request ($759.1 million): The increase of $38.6 million is primarily due to a $19.2 million increase in DOE/SC funding in HCSIA in support of the NSCI to develop scientific applications, particularly those advancing clean energy technologies, and to explore technologies "beyond Moore's Law;" a $14.8 million increase in the Energy Transformation Acceleration Fund for ARPA-E projects in HCSS; and smaller increases and decreases in other PCAs.

DARPA

Comparison of 2016 estimate ($425.5 million) and 2017 request ($440.4 million): The increase of $14.9 million is primarily due to a $27.6 million increase in LSN for Advanced RF Mapping and Spectrum Efficiency and Access programs, with smaller increases and decreases in other PCAs, partially offset by a decrease of $17.8 million in EHCS due to the completion of the Unconventional Processing of Signals for Intelligent Data Exploitation program.

NIST

Comparison of 2016 estimate ($146.9 million) and 2017 request ($160.5 million): The increase of $13.6 million is due to a $13.6 million increase in EHCS for the Measurement Science for Future Computing Technologies and Applications initiative.

NNSA
Comparison of 2016 estimate ($22.2 million) and 2017 request ($33.5 million): The increase of $11.3 million is due to an increase in exascale vendor R&D partnerships.

NITRD Program Budget Analysis by PCA

Using the information presented above, this section provides an analysis of the NITRD Program budget by PCA, summarizing the more substantial differences between 2016 estimates and 2017 requests. The changes are described below.

EHCS
Comparison of 2016 estimate ($680.7 million) and 2017 request ($647.5 million): The $33.2 million decrease is largely due to a decrease of $48.2 million at DoD and $17.8 million decrease at DARPA, partially offset by a $13.6 million increase at NIST, $11.3 million increase at DOE/NNSA, and smaller increases at other agencies.

HCI&IM
Comparison of 2016 estimate ($734.2 million) and 2017 request ($716.4 million): The $17.8 million decrease is largely due to a decrease of $12.7 million at DoD, with smaller increases and decreases at other agencies.

HCSIA
Comparison of 2016 estimate ($930.8 million) and 2017 request ($958.3 million): The $27.5 million increase is largely due to an increase of $19.2 million at DOE, with smaller increases and decreases at other agencies.

HCSS
Comparison of 2016 estimate ($155.0 million) and 2017 request ($167.5 million): The $12.5 million increase is largely due to an increase of $14.8 million at DOE, with smaller increases and decreases at other agencies.

LSN
Comparison of 2016 estimate ($323.4 million) and 2017 request ($386.4 million): The $63.0 million increase is largely due to an increase of $23.4 million at DoD, $27.6 million increase at DARPA, with smaller increases at other agencies.

Budget Request by Program Component Area

Cyber Security and Information Assurance (CSIA)

NITRD Agencies: DARPA, DHS, DoD (CERDEC), DoD Service Research Organizations (AFOSR, AFRL, ARL, ARO, ONR) DOE/OE, NIH, NIJ, NIST, NSA, NSF, and OSD
Other Participants: DOT, IARPA, NRC, ODNI, and Treasury

CSIA focuses on research and development to detect, prevent, resist, respond to, and recover from actions that compromise or threaten to compromise the availability, integrity, or confidentiality of computer- and network-based systems. These systems provide the IT foundation in every sector of the economy, including critical infrastructures such as power grids, financial systems, and air-traffic-control networks. These systems also support national defense, homeland security, and other Federal missions. Broad areas of emphasis include Internet and network security; security of information and computer-based systems; approaches to achieving hardware and software security; testing and assessment of computer-based systems security; reconstitution of computer-based systems and data; and resilience against cyber-attacks on computer-based systems that monitor, protect, and control critical infrastructure.

> **CSIA Coordination**: For the CSIA PCA, agencies coordinate their R&D activities through the Cyber Security and Information Assurance Interagency Working Group (CSIA IWG) and the Cyber Security and Information Assurance Research and Development Senior Steering Group (CSIA R&D SSG).

President's FY 2017 Request

Strategic Priorities Underlying This Request

High-level Federal strategic priorities for cybersecurity research are outlined in the 2011 *Trustworthy Cyberspace: Strategic Plan for the Federal Cybersecurity Research and Development Program*.[6] The priorities of the Strategic Plan are further refined and expanded by mission requirements of individual agencies. The role and guidance of the Strategic Plan have been reaffirmed by the OMB-OSTP Memorandum on Science and Technology Priorities for the FY 2017 Budget.[7] Future investments will be guided by the recently released *Federal Cybersecurity Research and Development Strategic Plan: Ensuring Prosperity and National Security*.[8]

The objectives for cybersecurity R&D are characterized by the following strategic directions:

- **Inducing Change** – Utilizing game-changing themes to direct efforts toward understanding the underlying root causes of known threats with the goal of disrupting the status quo; the research themes include Tailored Trustworthy Spaces, Moving Target, Cyber Economic Incentives, and Designed-In Security.

- **Assuring the Mission** – Advancing cyber-supported warfighting and non-military capabilities by developing technologies to be aware of missions and threats, compute optimal assurance solutions, and implement protection as needed via mission agility or infrastructure reinforcement.

- **Developing Scientific Foundations** – Developing an organized, cohesive scientific foundation to the body of knowledge that informs the field of cybersecurity through adoption of a systematic, rigorous, and disciplined scientific approach.

---

[6] *Trustworthy Cyberspace: Strategic Plan for the Federal Cybersecurity Research and Development Program*, December 2011, NSTC: http://www.whitehouse.gov/sites/default/files/microsites/ostp/fed_cybersecurity_rd_strategic_plan_2011.pdf.

[7] OMB-OSTP Memorandum on Science and Technology Priorities for the FY 2017 Budget (M-15-16), July 9, 2015: https://www.whitehouse.gov/sites/default/files/microsites/ostp/m-15-16.pdf.

[8] *Federal Cybersecurity Research and Development Strategic Plan: Ensuring Prosperity and National Security*. February 2016, NSTC: https://www.whitehouse.gov/sites/whitehouse.gov/files/documents/2016_Federal_Cybersecurity_Research_and_Development_Stratgeic_Plan.pdf.

- **Maximizing Research Impact** – Catalyzing integration across the research themes, cooperation between governmental and private-sector communities, collaboration across international borders, and strengthened linkages to other national priorities, such as health and energy.

- **Accelerating Transition to Practice** – Focusing efforts to ensure adoption and implementation of the new technologies and strategies that emerge from research and activities to build a scientific foundation so as to create measurable improvements in the cybersecurity landscape.

Highlights of Request

To address these strategic priorities, the CSIA agencies report the following topical areas as highlights of their planned R&D investments for FY 2017. Agencies are listed in alphabetical order:

- **Inducing change**

    Tailored Trustworthy Spaces theme: Enable flexible, adaptive, distributed trust environments that can support functional and policy requirements arising from a wide spectrum of user activities in the face of an evolving range of threats.

    - Cyber physical systems security – DHS, NIST, and NSF

    - High assurance security architectures – AFRL, DARPA, NIST, NSA, ONR, and OSD

    - IT Security Automation/Continuous Monitoring/Security Content Automation Protocol program – NIST and NSA

    - Operating Systems and Compilers for Heterogeneous (Multi-ISA) Computing; Rethinking Software Deployment and Customization for Improved Security and Efficiency – ONR

    - Secure wireless networking – ARL, ARO, CERDEC, DARPA, NSA, NSF, ONR, and OSD

    - Security for cloud-based systems – AFOSR, AFRL, DARPA, DHS, NIST, and NSF

    - Security for the Internet of Things (IoT) – DARPA, DHS, NSF, and NSA

    - Transparent computing – DARPA

    - Trusted foundation for defensive cyberspace operations – AFRL, ARL, ARO, CERDEC, ONR, and OSD

    Moving Target theme: Develop capabilities to create, analyze, evaluate, and deploy mechanisms and strategies that are diverse and continually shift and change over time to increase complexity and cost for attackers, limit the exposure of vulnerabilities and malicious opportunities, and increase resiliency.

    - Agile Resilient Embedded Systems; Automated Cyber Survivability – AFRL

    - Application Security Threat Attack Modeling (ASTAM) – DHS

    - Cyber Agility program – AFRL and OSD

    - Information Security Automation Program (ISAP) – DHS, NIST, and NSA

    - Moving Target Decoys and Disinformation (CyberMoat); Investigation on Automated Composition for Technical Document – ONR

    - Moving Target Defense program – DHS

    - Proactive and Reactive Adaptive Systems – NSA

    - Security Automation and Vulnerability Management – NIST

    - Tactical Cyber Situational Awareness – ARL

Cyber Economic Incentives theme: Develop effective market-based, legal, regulatory, or institutional incentives to make cybersecurity ubiquitous, including incentives affecting individuals and organizations.

- Cyber Economics Incentives Research program – DHS

Designed-in Security theme: Develop capabilities to design and evolve high-assurance, software-intensive systems reliably while managing risk, cost, schedule, quality, and complexity. Create tools and environments that enable the simultaneous development of cyber-secure systems and the associated assurance evidence necessary to prove the system's resistance to vulnerabilities, flaws, and attacks.

- Autonomic Computing; Machine Assisted Software Development – ONR
- Roots of Trust – AFRL, NIST, and NSA
- SafeWare; Space/Time Analysis for Cybersecurity (STAC); Vetting Commodity IT Software and Firmware (VET) – DARPA
- Software Assurance Metrics And Tool Evaluation (SAMATE) – NIST
- Static Tool Analysis Modernization Project (STAMP) – DHS
- Trusted Computing – AFRL, NSA, and OSD

Cross-cutting all themes:

- Secure and Trustworthy Cyberspace (SaTC) program – NSF
- Cybersecurity for Energy Delivery Systems (CEDS) program – DOE/OE
- Embedded, Mobile, Tactical Systems security – OSD and DHS
- Leveraging the Analog Domain for Security (LADS) – DARPA

- **Assuring the Mission**

  Provide the ability to avoid, fight through, survive, and recover from cyber threats.

  - Application Security Threat Attack Modeling (ASTAM) – DHS
  - Assuring Effective Missions; Resilient Infrastructure – OSD
  - Cyber-Based Mission Assurance on Trust-Enhanced Hardware (CMATH); Mission Awareness for Mission Assurance (MAMA); Autonomous Defensive Cyber Operations (ADCO); Secure Cyber Resilient Unmanned Aerial System Missions (SCRUM) – AFRL
  - Edge-Directed Cyber Technologies for Reliable Mission Communication; Extreme DDoS Defense; Cyber Fault-tolerant Attack Recovery (CFAR); Plan X – DARPA
  - Resilient and Agile Cyber Defenses for Tactical Mobile – ARL
  - Techniques and Middleware for Robust Control Systems Design on Single- and Multi-Core Architectures; Enhancing Fault Tolerant System into Cyber-Attack Tolerant for ICS (CPS) – ONR

- **Developing Scientific Foundations**

  Science of Security: In anticipation of the challenges in securing the cyber systems of the future, the Federal research in the areas of science of security aims to develop an organized, scientific foundation that informs the cybersecurity domain, by organizing disparate areas of knowledge, enabling discovery of universal laws, and by applying the rigor of the scientific method.

  - Adversarial and Uncertain Reasoning for Adaptive Cyber Defense – ARO

- Cyber measurement and experimentation – OSD

- Cyber-Security Collaborative Research Alliance (Cyber CRA); Network Science Collaborative Technology Alliance (CTA) – ARL

- Non-Equilibrium Dynamic Cyber-Interaction; Multidisciplinary University Research Initiative (MURI) on Practical and Realistic Dynamic Formalism for Advanced Cyber Interaction; Situational Awareness through Network Science – ONR

- Science for Cybersecurity (S4C) – ARL and ARO

- Secure and Trustworthy Cyberspace (SaTC) program – NSF

Cross-cutting foundations:

- Cryptography – DARPA, NIST, NSA, NSF, and ONR

- Models, standards, testing, and metrics – ARL, ARO, DHS, DOE/OE, NIST, NSF, and OSD

- Foundations of Trust – AFRL, ARL, ARO, CERDEC, DARPA, DOE/OE, NIST, NSA, NSF, ONR, and OSD

- Security Management and Assurance Standards – NIST

- Quantum information science and technology – AFRL, DOE/OE, IARPA, NIST, and ONR

- Cybersecurity education – DHS, NIST, and NSF

- **Maximizing Research Impact**

  Supporting national priorities: The cybersecurity research themes provide a framework for addressing the cybersecurity R&D requirements associated with national priorities in, for example, the healthcare, energy, financial services, and defense sectors.

  - Cybersecurity Education and Workforce Development – DHS, NIST, and NSF

  - Health IT Security Program; National Strategy for Trusted Identities in Cyberspace (NSTIC); Privacy Engineering Initiative; Standards Framework for Critical Infrastructure Protection (Executive Order 13636, "Improving Critical Infrastructure Cybersecurity") – NIST

  - Journal of Sensitive Cybersecurity Research and Engineering (JSCoRE) – ODNI

  - National Critical Infrastructure Security and Resilience R&D Plan (Presidential Policy Directive 21, "Critical Infrastructure Security and Resilience") – DHS and DOE/OE

  - Rapid Attack Detection, Isolation and Characterization Systems (RADICS) – DARPA

  - Smart Grid Interoperability Panel - Smart Grid Cybersecurity Committee – DOE/OE and NIST

- **Accelerating Transition to Practice**

  Technology discovery, evaluation, transition, adoption, and commercialization: Explicit, coordinated processes that transition the fruits of research into practice to achieve significant, long-lasting impact.

  - Center for Advanced Communications; National Cybersecurity Center of Excellence (NCCoE) – NIST

  - Cybersecurity for Energy Delivery Systems (CEDS) program – DOE/OE

  - Cybersecurity research infrastructure - Defense Technology Experimental Research (DETER) testbed, Protected Repository for the Defense of Infrastructure Against Cyber Threats (PREDICT), Software Assurance Marketplace (SWAMP); Information Technology Security Entrepreneurs' Forum (ITSEF); Transition to Practice program – DHS

- DoD Cyber Transition to Practice Initiative – OSD

- NSA Technology Transfer Program (TTP) – NSA

- Secure and Trustworthy Cyberspace (SaTC) program – NSF

- Small Business Innovative Research (SBIR) conferences – DoD, DHS, and NSF

- Testbeds and infrastructure for R&D – DARPA, DHS, NSF, and OSD

Planning and Coordination Supporting Request

The CSIA agencies engage in a variety of cooperative efforts – from implementing multiagency testbeds essential for experimentation with new technologies at realistic scales, to collaborative deployment of prototypes, to common standards. The following is a representative summary of current multiagency collaborations:

- **Co-funding**: Defense Technology Experimental Research (DETER) testbed – DHS and NSF; National Centers of Academic Excellence in Information Assurance Education and Research – DHS and NSA

- **Collaborative research**: Cyber-Security Collaborative Research Alliance (CRA) – ARL; Cyber Forensics Working Group – DHS law enforcement components, DoD, FBI, and NIST; NSF/Intel Partnership on Cyber-Physical Systems Security and Privacy – NSF and Intel Corp.; Secure, Trustworthy, Assured and Resilient Semiconductors and Systems (STARSS) – NSF and Semiconductor Research Corporation (SRC); SEI Cyber Research – OSD and Software Engineering Institute; Nanoscale hardware security – AFOSR, NNCO, and SRC

- **Workshops**: Cyber-Physical Systems Public Working Group Workshops – NIST; Cryptographic Key Management Workshop – NIST; Software and Supply Chain Assurance Forum – NIST; Cybersecurity Applications and Technology Conference for Homeland Security – DHS; Small Business Innovation Research (SBIR) Conference – DHS, NIST, and OSD; Annual IT Security Automation Conference – DHS, NIST, and NSA; National Initiative for Cybersecurity Education Annual Workshop – DHS, NIST, NSA, NSF, and OSD; Cloud Forums – DHS, GSA, and NIST; Mobile Security Forum – NIST and NSA; IT Security Entrepreneur Forum, Innovation Summit, SINET Showcase, Transition To Practice Showcase, Research and Development Showcase and Technical Workshop – DHS; Workshops on Incorporating Security Concepts in Undergraduate Computer Science Curriculum, Formal Methods and Security – NSF; International Conference on Software Security and Reliability – NIST; Computational Cybersecurity in Compromised Environments (C3E) Workshops – ODNI

- **Collaborative deployment**: Cyber-Physical Systems Global City Teams Challenge / SmartAmerica – NIST; DNS security (DNSSEC) and routing security – AFRL, DHS, and NIST; The National Vulnerability Database – DHS and NIST; U.S. Government Configuration Baseline (USGCB) – NIST and NSA

- **Technical standards**: Developing, maintaining, and coordinating validation programs for cryptographic standards – NIST and NSA; participation in Internet Engineering Task Force security groups to develop standard representations reference implementations of security-relevant data – DHS, NIST, NSA, and OSD; Smart Grid Interoperability Panel - Smart Grid Cybersecurity Committee – DOE/OE and NIST

- **Testbeds**: Continued joint development of research testbeds, such as DETER, Protected Repository for the Defense of Infrastructure Against Cyber Threats (PREDICT), Distributed Environment for Critical Infrastructure Decision-making Exercises (DECIDE), Wisconsin Advanced Internet Laboratory (WAIL), Mobile Networks Testbed Emulation – ARL, ARO, CERDEC, DHS, DOE/OE, NSF, ONR, and Treasury

- **DoD Cyber Community of Interest (COI)**: Oversight and coordination of all defensive cyber S&T programs – DARPA, DoD Service research organizations, and OSD

- **Technical Cooperation Program Communications, Command, Control and Intelligence (C3I) Group**: Information assurance and defensive information warfare – AFRL, ARL, ARO, CERDEC, NSA, ONR, and OSD

- **International collaboration**: NSF and the U.S.-Israel Binational Science Foundation joint program; NSF and the Netherlands Organization for Scientific Research; NSF and Brazil Ministry of Science Technology and Innovation; U.S. Army-United Kingdom Network and Information Sciences International Technology Alliance; DHS international engagements and co-funding activities with Australia, Canada, Germany, Israel, Netherlands, Sweden, United Kingdom, European Union, and Japan.

- **Cyber education**: Centers of Academic Excellence – NSA; CyberCorps: Scholarship for Service, Advanced Technological Education (ATE) – NSF; National Initiative for Cybersecurity Education (NICE) – DHS, NIST, NSA, NSF, ODNI, and OSD; Cybersecurity Competitions – DHS; Cybersecurity Organizational/Operational Learning (COOL) – DHS

Additional 2016 and 2017 Activities by Agency

The following list provides a summary of individual agencies' ongoing programmatic interests for 2016 and 2017 under the CSIA PCA:

- **AFRL**: Secure systems foundations; foundations for trusted architectures; cyber agility (configuration-based moving target defense, polymorphic enclaves, IP hopping, cyber deception); mission-centric cyber assurance (mission assurance in the cloud, data hiding and analysis, threat abatement, assured resources); Assured by Design (self-regenerative architecture, science of mission assurance, domain modification, engineering assured systems); nanoscale security.

- **ARL, ARO, and CERDEC**: Communication and electronic warfare hardware/software convergence security; software-defined radio protection; software/hardware assurance; cyber cognition; trusted social computing; cyber situational awareness; trust, decision making, and influence in multi-genre networks; fundamentals of intrusion understanding and avoidance; authentication and access control; lightweight high assurance data-at-rest/data-in-transit solutions; automated malware analysis; unconventional communications networks (quantum networks, cognitive hybrid networking); cyber lab and field-based risk reduction testing.

- **DARPA**: Information Assurance and Survivability (core computing and networking technologies to protect DoD's information infrastructure and mission-critical information systems; tools and methods to uncover hidden malicious functionality; algorithms for detecting anomalous and threat-related behaviors; and techniques applicable to U.S. critical infrastructure, e.g., the power grid).

- **DHS**: Cyber transition and outreach (Transition to Practice [TTP]); network and system security integration (security for cloud-based systems, mobile device security, cybersecurity for law enforcement, data privacy and identity management, software quality assurance, usable security and security metrics); trustworthy cyberinfrastructure (Internet measurement and attack modeling, process control system security, secure protocols, distributed denial of service defense); cybersecurity user protection and education (cybersecurity competitions, cybersecurity forensics, data privacy technologies, identity management); cyber-physical systems security (automotive, medical, building controls, aviation, maritime).

- **DOE/OE**: Continue to align research activities with the DOE-facilitated, energy sector-led *Roadmap to Achieve Energy Delivery Systems Cybersecurity*, updated in 2011, strategic framework and vision that, by 2020, resilient energy delivery systems are designed, installed, operated, and maintained to survive a cyber-incident while sustaining critical functions.

- **IARPA**: Cyber-attack Automated Unconventional Sensor Environment (CAUSE); Trusted Integrated Chips (TIC).

- **NIH**: Research in access and privacy for medical and electronic health records; particular interest includes automated and remote access, standards, and protection of records.

- **NIST**: Foundations (risk management, identity management, key management, security automation, vulnerability management, cryptography); security overlays (healthcare, Smart Grid, cyber-physical systems, public safety networks, trusted identities); security and mobility; continuous monitoring; biometrics; Security Content Automation Protocol; security for cloud computing; security for electronic voting; usable security; supply chain risk management; Big Data Initiative; participation in standards development organizations; techniques for measuring security; metrology infrastructure for modeling and simulation; privacy engineering.

- **NSA**: Trusted computing (high assurance security architectures enabled by virtualization, improved enterprise protection through strong software measurement and reporting); secure mobility; systems behavior.

- **NSF**: Secure and Trustworthy Cyberspace (SaTC) program: a joint program by the NSF Directorates of Computer and Information Science and Engineering (CISE), Mathematical and Physical Sciences (MPS), Social, Behavioral and Economic Sciences (SBE), Education and Human Resources (EHR), and Engineering (ENG) covering all aspects of cybersecurity research and education.

- **ONR**: Cybersecurity and real-time system theory; machine-assisted situational awareness and planning; real-time virtual machines and real-time cloud provisioning; cyber information infrastructure (resilient autonomic computing, dynamically reconfigurable computing systems, data science, data security, software science, tactical cloud, SOA and beyond, quantum computing, bio / analog computing); proactive cyber-physical system defense.

- **OSD**: Cyber Applied Research program (developing new security methods to integrate Service Laboratory and NSA research for new joint capabilities); assuring effective missions (cyber mission control, effects at scale); cyber agility (autonomic cyber agility, cyber maneuver); cyber resilience (resilient architectures, resilient algorithms and protocols); foundations of trust (system-level trust, trustworthy components and mechanisms); modeling, simulation, and experimentation; embedded, mobile, and tactical; cybersecurity metrics; DoD Cyber Transition to Practice Initiative; and SBIR program and workshop to foster innovation and facilitate networking with small businesses.

Enabling-R&D for High-Capability Computing Systems (EHCS)

NITRD Agencies: DARPA, DoD (HPCMP), DoD Service Research Organizations, DOE/NNSA, DOE/SC, EPA, NASA, NIH, NIST, NOAA, NSA, and NSF
Other Participants: IARPA

High-capability computing systems (HCS) enable modern scientific exploration and insights across a broad spectrum from astronomy to advanced combustion engine manufacturing, hurricane prediction, nuclear physics, petroleum exploration, and further understanding of the human brain. The R&D that enables HCS addresses many of society's long-term challenges and strongly contributes to strengthening the Nation's security and leadership in science, engineering, and technology. Agencies involved in EHCS conduct and coordinate R&D to enable advancements in high-capability computing systems, including the hardware, software, architecture, system performance, computational algorithms, data analytics, development tools, and software methods for extreme data- and compute-intensive workloads and to develop fundamentally new approaches to high-capability computing systems. The goals of these R&D efforts are to enable the successful development and effective use of future high-capability systems and to drive solutions in support of national security, economic competitiveness, cutting-edge science, engineering, and projected Federal agency mission needs.

Research areas of interest under EHCS include promising future computational technologies such as quantum information science, superconducting supercomputing, and biological computing; parallel programming environments that increase developer productivity and ability to program at scale; system software, applications, and system architectures that effectively utilize up to billion-way concurrency; reducing computing system energy consumption by orders of magnitude; achieving system resilience at embedded and extreme scales; heterogeneous accelerated and scalable systems for extreme performance; and enabling future revolutions in simulation, data analytics, and big-data-enabled applications and technology.

> **EHCS Coordination**: For the EHCS PCA, agencies coordinate their R&D activities through the High End Computing Interagency Working Group (HEC IWG).

President's FY 2017 Request

Strategic Priorities Underlying This Request

For decades, EHCS agencies have led development of increasingly capable computing technologies, user environments, and applications that have impacted the entire computing industry. These advances not only enhanced Federal mission success, but also enabled and motivated increased high-capability computing system usage by industry and academia that has promoted economic competitiveness, national security, and scientific leadership. Thus, continued innovation by EHCS agencies holds promise for tremendous benefits to the Nation. However, the HCS community faces great challenges in creating effective high-capability computing systems using technology that is driven primarily by the consumer marketplace, and in building collaborative approaches to combine the best features of the Internet and big data computing with traditional supercomputing. New high-capability systems will require significant advances in energy efficiency, data transport, concurrency, resiliency, security, and programmability. These challenges must be met to achieve and exploit the orders-of-magnitude increase in HCS capabilities that are needed to solve increasingly data-intensive and complex problems for science, engineering, manufacturing, and national security. To address the growing complexity and long-term costs of emerging platforms, HCS researchers seek to exploit heterogeneous advanced processor technologies, novel memory and storage technologies, and innovative approaches to software creation, and to provide innovative solutions for energy consumption, reliability, and scalability. Given these challenges and opportunities, the EHCS agencies see the following as key research priorities for FY 2017:

- **Extreme-scale computation**: Integrate computer science and applied mathematical foundations to address the challenges of productive and efficient computation from the embedded through the exascale level and beyond. Develop innovative systems that combine increased speed, efficient use of energy, data centric techniques, economic viability, high productivity, and robustness to meet future agency needs for systems that manage and analyze ultra-large volumes of data and run multi-scale, multidisciplinary science and engineering simulations and national security applications. Explore new concepts and approaches for solving technical challenges such as power consumption, efficient data placement and utilization, heterogeneous domain-specific performance acceleration, thermal management, file system I/O bottlenecks, resiliency, highly parallel system architectures with support for up to billion-way concurrency, and programming language and software development environments that can increase the usability and utility of large-scale multiprocessor (including hybrid) systems. Develop, test, and evaluate prototype HCS technologies, systems, and software to reduce industry and end-user risk and to increase technological competitiveness. Implement critical technology R&D partnerships for extreme-scale readiness.

- **New directions in HCS hardware, software, computer science, and system architectures**: Develop novel scientific frameworks, power-efficient system architectures, heterogeneous and specialized system acceleration, programming environments, measurement science, thermal management, and hardware and software prototypes to take computing performance and communications "beyond Moore's Law" and to advance potential new breakthroughs in biological, quantum, and superconducting computing.

- **Productivity**: Continued research and development of new metrics of system performance, including benchmarking; workflow systems and software to enable, support, and increase the productivity of geographically dispersed collaborative teams that develop future HCS applications; and new methods of programming that extend and enhance usability and programmability of high-capability computing systems.

- **Broadening impact**: Conduct crosscutting activities by the EHCS agencies, individually or collectively, that span multiple major priorities and serve to extend the breadth and impact of high-capability computing to meet the Nation's highest science, engineering, national security, and competitiveness priorities, including expanding the workforce for high-capability computing systems.

Highlights of the Request

The EHCS agencies report the following areas as highlights of their planned research investments for FY 2017 under each of the main EHCS priorities. Agencies are listed in alphabetical order:

- **Extreme-scale computation**

  o **DOE/NNSA**: Investment in critical R&D technologies to ensure high, sustained application performance on incoming production systems: Trinity (40 PF) and Sierra (150 PF). Co-design on performance impacts of applications by advanced architectures via proxy apps, abstraction layers, task-based programming models, resilience techniques, burst buffers, etc.

  o **DOE/SC**: Exascale Computing Project – Conduct research, development, and design efforts in hardware and software, and mathematical technologies leading toward capable exascale systems; partner with HPC vendors to accelerate the pace of the implementation of technologies required for capable exascale computing; prepare today's scientific and data-intensive computing applications to exploit fully the capabilities of exascale systems by coordinating their development with the emerging technologies from research, development, and design efforts. Other research includes computer science research that focuses on data-intensive science challenges and on tools, user interfaces, HPC software stacks for development and execution that dynamically deal with time-varying energy efficiency and reliability requirements—including operating systems, file systems, compilers, and performance tools—and visualization and analytics tools that scale to extremely massive datasets. Continue support for Scientific Discovery through Advanced Computing (SciDAC) Institutes.

- o **EPA**: Develop novel approaches and techniques in environmental modeling addressing extreme-scale issues and challenges.

- o **NASA**: Focus on building up the knowledge base at NASA computing centers on extreme-scale computing application programming models.

- o **NIH**: Helping to unravel life's mystery through development of new computation methods and novel approaches to data analysis at the extreme scale; development of advanced computer hardware for biomedical simulations.

- **New directions in HCS hardware, software, computer science, and system architectures**

  - o **AFOSR**: Research on multicore technologies to provide new capabilities that unify high-capability computing systems with real-time, data-acquisition and control; research on computational mathematics and algorithms for new methods of modeling dynamically integrated large-scale big data and large-scale big computing under the Dynamic Data Driven Applications Systems (DDDAS) program.

  - o **DoD (HPCMP)**: Augment stable, large-scale HPC systems with targeted exploratory or emerging computational platforms to address DoD's emerging computational use cases in science and technology, data analysis for decision support and acquisition engineering analysis; develop scalable, complex, multi-physics-based codes for critical defense applications on next-generation supercomputers; develop advanced cybersecurity tools and instrumentation.

  - o **DOE/NNSA**: Investments in identified R&D critical technologies to address extreme-scale barriers via R&D collaboration with DOE/SC.

  - o **DOE/SC**: Continued research to support data-intensive science, especially where challenges overlap those for exascale; machine learning for adaptive systems and analytics; cybersecurity.

  - o **EPA**: Support robust mission-related research program with focus on next-generation deployments, developing both tools and techniques for environmental sciences.

  - o **IARPA**: Research in superconducting supercomputing including cryogenic memory. New approaches to enable high performance computing systems with greatly improved memory capacity and energy efficiency; logic, communications and systems; development of advanced superconducting circuits and integration with memory and other components.

  - o **NASA**: Research, explore, and exploit alternative HCS architectures such as quantum computing systems, including quantum algorithms for hard, discrete optimization problems and their mapping to and embedding on quantum architectures; Small Business Innovation Research (SBIR) projects in efficient computing, user productivity environments, and ultra-sale computing.

  - o **NIST**: Measurement science and technology for future computing and communication technologies - quantum information science and engineering; quantum information theory (quantum algorithms, complexity: assessing the true power of quantum resources); quantum computing assessment (techniques and tools to assess the capabilities of candidate technologies); quantum technology demonstrations (evaluating feasibility of applications of quantum resources in computing, communications); developing numerical methods, algorithms and software that are robust and reliable for future advanced computing systems; providing standards for interoperability involving large and often heterogeneous datasets; unravelling the complexities that exist in materials science and engineering data, to provide new and valuable information not available by other approaches.

  - o **NOAA**: Research in modeling techniques for heterogeneous computing systems; explore next generation of fine-grained architecture computing methods; improve speed, accuracy, integrity of data transfer for large datasets; big data science, tools, and techniques for earth and environmental sciences;

research to improve models for hurricane forecasts, weather, climate change, ecosystems, and Earth Systems Modeling Framework (ESMF).

- o **NSA**: Research for analytic and exploitation computing - superconducting supercomputing; quantum computing; probabilistic and neuromorphic computing; high performance data analytics; explore innovative solutions that meet the challenges of tomorrow for energy, productivity, and resilience of HCS systems.

- o **NSF**: Quantum and biological computing; research with emphasis to support models for potential future national-scale, network-aware, data-aware cyberinfrastructure attributes, approaches, and capabilities under the programs CC*DNI (Campus Cyberinfrastructure - Data, Networking, and Innovation [CC*DNI]) and IRNC (International Research Network Connections). CIF21 (Cyberinfrastructure Framework for 21st Century Science and Engineering) programs to accelerate research and education and new functional capabilities in computational and data-intensive science and engineering. CIF21 programs include the NSF Big Data Initiative for advancing the foundation of big data science and engineering; Computational and Data-Enabled Science and Engineering (CDS&E) meta-program for developing new computation and data analysis approaches to advance major cross-cutting or disciplinary breakthroughs; and EarthCube for developing transformative concepts for creating integrated data infrastructure across the geosciences. Other programs include Understanding the Brain (UtB) – research into multi-scale computational models and data analysis from molecular to behavioral; Innovations at the Nexus of Food, Energy, and Water Systems (INFEWS) – research into large-scale data analysis, including modeling and simulation, and optimization of complex systems.

- o **OSD**: Extending abstractions in the Parallel Boost Graph Library (PBGL) to support a more complete set of graph algorithms on GPUs, work to be performed at the Software Engineering Institute (SEI).

- **Productivity**

  - o **DoD, DOE/SC, and NSF**: Capabilities for scientific research including computational concepts, methods, and tools for discovery. Centers, institutes, and partnerships for predictive and data-intensive science; applied math and computer science challenges of data-intensive science and scientific computing at extreme scale.

  - o **DOE/NNSA**: Continue development of and pursue community adoption of High Performance Conjugate Gradient (HPCG) benchmark as a complement to Linpack benchmark for the Top 500 list.

  - o **NIST**: Provide leadership and guidance for cloud computing paradigms in order to catalyze its use within industry and government; develop interoperability, portability, and security standards for cloud computing.

  - o **NSA**: System level metrics for energy, productivity, and resilience.

  - o **NSF**: Benchmark of Realistic Scientific Application Performance (BRAP) of large-scale computing systems.

- **Broadening impact**

  - o **DoD (HPCMP)**: Develop next-generation computational workforce within DoD through the HPC Internship Program and User Productivity Enhancement, Technology Transfer and Training (PETTT) Program.

  - o **NASA:** Expand the utilization of HCS in Model Based System Engineering (MBSE) and Observation System Simulation Experiments (OSSE); support next-generation application workforce development through NASA Earth and Space Science Fellowship (NESSF) program.

  - o **NSF:** Blue Waters – graduate fellowship, student internship, virtual school, etc.

Planning and Coordination Supporting Request

Coordination among the HEC IWG agencies focuses on computer science advancements to improve the performance and efficiency of the current generation of HCS hardware and software as well as on avenues of fundamental research to create revolutionary new architectures and systems. The complexity of high-end hardware architectures, systems software, and supporting technologies is such that Federal program managers and researchers depend on the constant flow of information among colleagues and technical experts to keep current with developments, gain new knowledge, and share best practices and lessons learned. In addition to joint technical/planning workshops and proposal/technical reviews that HEC IWG agencies routinely conduct, the following are selected examples of the scope of interagency collaboration under each of the EHCS strategic priorities:

- **Extreme-scale computation**

  - **Joint workshops on extreme-scale resilience**: DoD, DOE/NNSA, and DOE/SC

  - **DOE intra-agency collaborations**: Critical R&D investments in memory, processors, storage, interconnects, systems engineering, etc.; joint development work to fully address the parallelism, power, memory, and data movement issues associated with multicore computing at the exascale level; collaboration on all aspects of the Exascale Computing Initiative (ECI)/ Exascale Computing Project (ECP) – DOE/NNSA and DOE/SC

  - **Computing MOU:** DoD, DOE/NNSA, and DOE/SC

  - **Extreme-scale R&D technologies and Modeling/Simulation Working Group:** HEC IWG agencies

  - **Big data:** Explore synergies and convergences between HCS and the big data realm to ensure HCS capabilities support the many emerging data-intensive applications and domains (e.g., sponsor panel at Supercomputing conference on convergence of big data and HCS)– HEC IWG and BD SSG agencies

- **Broad applicability and use of capable exascale computing**: Collaboration with other Federal agencies for broad use and applicability of exascale computing (e.g., joint Request for Information [RFI] by DOE, NIH, and NSF on science drivers requiring capable exascale HPC developed for NSCI) – HEC IWG and other agencies

- **New directions in HCS hardware, software, computer science, and system architectures**

  - **Quantum information theory and science**: Study information, communication, and computation based on devices governed by the principles of quantum physics – DOE/NNSA, DOE/SC, IARPA, NASA, NIST, NSA, and NSF

  - **Superconducting (cryogenic) supercomputing:** IARPA and NSA

  - **Cloud-based HCS**: Explore supercomputing in the cloud through public and private service providers to determine applicability and efficiencies for subset of Federal HCS needs – NASA, NIH, and NSF

  - **Extreme-scale system software R&D co-funding**: DOE/NNSA, and DOE/SC

  - **3-D stacked memory**: DOE/NNSA and DOE/SC

  - **Memory and machine learning program**: IARPA, DOE/SC, and NSA

  - **Source code porting and scaling studies**: Collaborations for weather and climate models – NASA, NOAA, and NSF (TACC)

  - **Other beyond Moore's Law computing technologies research**: DOE/NNSA, DOE/SC, NIST, NSA, and NSF

- **Productivity**

  - **Benchmarking and performance modeling**: Collaborate on developing performance measurement test cases with applications commonly used by the Federal HCS community for use in system procurements, evaluation of Federal HCS system productivity – DoD (HPCMP), DOE/NNSA, DOE/SC, NASA, NSA, and NSF

  - **HCS metrics**: Coordinate on effective metrics for application development and execution on high-end systems – DoD, DOE/NNSA, DOE/SC, NASA, NSA, and NSF

- **Broadening impact**

  - **HCS hardware and software**: Facilitate access to and share knowledge gained and lessons learned from HCS hardware and software development efforts – DoD, DOE/NNSA, DOE/SC, NASA, NIST, NOAA, and NSF

  - **HCS tools**: Coordinate R&D in operating and runtime systems, development environments, productivity tools, languages, compilers, libraries – DOD (HPCMP), DOE/NNSA, DOE/SC, NASA, NSA, and NSF

  - **HCS data challenges**: Coordinate with NITRD HCI&IM CG, LSN CG, and Big Data SSG and IWG on Digital Data – HEC IWG agencies

  - **NSCI**: Support a range of next-generation simulations and large-scale analytics to lower the barrier for scientists addressing a broad array of discovery challenges that require large-scale computation – NSF; support ongoing interagency implementation of NSCI and participation in cross-agency steering group – HEC IWG agencies and other agencies

Additional 2016 and 2017 Activities by Agency

The following list provides a summary of individual agencies' ongoing programmatic interests for 2016 and 2017 under the EHCS PCA:

- **AFOSR and NSF**: Multiagency solicitation on "InfoSymbiotic Systems," an expansion of the DDDAS program.

- **DARPA**: Develop computing technologies to enable processing of video and imagery based on the physics of nanoscale devices and probabilistic inference embedded within a digital system.

- **DoD (HPCMP)**: Research and development to address select RDT&E gaps in algorithms, application codes, and frameworks; applied research and new tools, through engagement with academic and other industry principal investigators, addressing five technical focus areas – highly scalable algorithms, exploitation of emerging accelerator hardware, multi-scale approaches, parallel I/O, and scalable parallel mesh generation.

- **DOE/SC**: Workshops on data management, analysis, and visualization for experimental and observational data; relationships among experimental, observational, and simulation data requirements; data provenance; and beyond Moore's Law: neuromorphic computing, quantum computing, etc. Exploratory Research for Extreme Scale Science (EXPRESS) announcements forthcoming; potential FOA in cybersecurity; scientific data management, analysis, and visualization for extreme-scale science, programming environments, operating and runtime systems, etc.

- **EPA**: Address extreme-scale, mission-related issues by focusing on analytics and computer science required in air quality, emissions, climate research, and interactions with human health.

- **NASA**: Complete the climate model downscaling experiments using high resolution regional climate models; invest in model output data analysis system software; continue to develop applications using quantum annealing processor.

- **NIST**: Quantum information theory (algorithms for simulation of quantum field theories; analysis of quantum cryptographic devices); quantum computing assessment (randomized benchmarks for testing fidelity of multi-qubit gates; quantum state tomography; efficient/reliable quantification of experimental results of Bell test); quantum technology demonstrations (develop/assess quantum memory/communications interface technologies; develop specialized quantum devices, e.g., random bit generators whose values are certified to be unknown before measurement).

- **NOAA**: Continue collaborative involvement with Earth Systems Modeling Framework (ESMF); improve techniques for transitioning codes from research to operations.

- **NSA**: SME collaborations (machine learning, file I/O, runtime systems, memory, and storage, etc.); system level metrics for energy, productivity, and resilience.

- **NSF**: XSEDE integrating services (coordination and management service, extended collaborative support service, training, education, and outreach service).

High-Capability Computing Systems Infrastructure and Applications (HCSIA)

NITRD Agencies: DoD (HPCMP), DoD Service Research Organizations, DOE/SC, NASA, NIH, NIST, NOAA, NSF, and OSD

The Federal high-capability computing systems (HCS) infrastructure is essential to diverse initiatives associated with critical national priorities including cybersecurity, understanding the human brain, big data, climate science, nanotechnology, the Materials Genome Initiative, and advanced manufacturing. Agencies investing in HCSIA coordinate Federal activities to provide HCS platforms and associated application software, communications, storage, data management, and HCS infrastructure to meet agency mission needs and support national competitiveness. Agencies invest individually and together to acquire and operate advanced supercomputing systems, applications software, extreme-scale data management and analysis, and advanced networking infrastructure and testbeds. This Federal HCS infrastructure enables researchers in academia, industry, Federally Funded Research and Development Centers (FFRDCs), and government institutions to model and simulate complex processes and analyze extreme-scale data over a broad spectrum of disciplines in national security, science, engineering, and industrial design and development. Advances in HCS technologies ultimately impact the entire spectrum of computing devices, from the largest systems to hand-held devices, allowing the most powerful computing platforms to become more affordable and smaller devices more capable over time.

> **HCSIA Coordination**: For the HCSIA PCA, agencies coordinate their R&D activities through the High End Computing Interagency Working Group (HEC IWG). Agencies may also coordinate through the Large Scale Networking Coordinating Group (LSN CG) on crosscutting topics or activities related to large-scale networking infrastructure in support of high-capability computing. For clarity, the association of a particular NITRD group with a particular coordination activity that crosscuts PCAs is provided below, as needed.

President's FY 2017 Request

Strategic Priorities Underlying this Request

Investments in Federal HCS facilities and infrastructure, advanced applications, and next-generation computing technologies and systems provide the means for industry, academia, and Federal laboratories to apply advanced computational capabilities in support of Federal agencies' diverse science, engineering, and national security missions. They also provide the government with the flexibility and expertise to meet new challenges as they emerge and to support national competitiveness. Priorities include:

- **Leadership-class and production high-capability computing systems**: Provide high-capability computing systems with capabilities and capacities needed to meet critical agency mission needs and support the national science and engineering research communities, U.S. industry, and academic research; ensure that emerging computer technologies support industrial, national security, and scientific applications and reduce energy requirements for and climate impact of computing technology at all scales. U.S. leadership in HCS is critical for maintaining U.S. competitiveness as a growing number of nations around the world increase their investments to develop and deploy indigenous high-capability computing systems and applications, threatening U.S. computing industries.

- **Advancement of high-capability computing systems applications**: Support the computational requirements of disciplines including national security, financial modeling, aerospace, astronomy, biology, biomedical science, chemistry, climate and weather, ecological computation, geodynamics, energy and environmental sciences, materials science, measurement science, nanoscale science and technology, physics, and other areas to make breakthrough scientific and technological discoveries and address national priorities. Develop scientific and engineering algorithms and applications software and tools for current and next-generation

HCS platforms; develop mission-responsive computational environments; and lead critical applied research in algorithms and software for emerging architectures in order to preserve the performance of existing codes.

- **High-capability computing systems infrastructure**: Provide efficient, effective, and dependable access to HCS facilities and resources, including testbeds, for user communities across a wide variety of skills and backgrounds in industry, academia, and Federal institutions; develop capabilities and enhance infrastructure for computational and data-enabled science, modeling, simulation, and analysis; and share best practices for managing and enhancing HCS resources in a cost-effective and energy-efficient manner.

- **Productivity**: Share lessons learned for acquisition; reduce total ownership costs of high-capability computing systems; integrate resources for improved productivity among all users; and increase science and engineering throughputs at HCS centers. Design and develop requirements for energy efficient HCS centers and integrate the requirement in acquisitions. Design and develop collaborative work environments, including data storage and management, accompany with high-speed network and storage to enable high-capability simulation and data analytics.

- **Broadening impact**: Conduct crosscutting activities by HCSIA agencies, individually or collectively, that span multiple major priorities and serve to extend the breadth and impact of high-capability computing to meet the Nation's highest science, engineering, national security, and competitiveness priorities.

Highlights of the Request

HCSIA agencies report the following areas as highlights of their planned investments for FY 2017 under each of the main HCSIA priorities. Agencies are listed in alphabetical order:

- **Leadership-class and production high-capability computing systems**

  - **DoD (HPCMP)**: Provide large capacity and capable HPC systems, application support, data analysis and visualization, and HPC system expertise to the DoD S&T, test and evaluation, and acquisition engineering communities.

  - **DOE/SC**: Acquire and operate increasingly capable computing systems, starting with multi-petaflop machines that incorporate emerging technologies from research investments. Site preparation activities will continue for 75 PF - 200 PF upgrades at each Leadership Computing Facility; Argonne LCF (ALCF) will also deploy an 8 PF - 10 PF system in FY 2017 to transition ALCF users to the new many-core architecture being introduced by computer vendors in that time frame; National Energy Research Scientific Computing Center (NERSC) will begin operation of the NERSC-8, which will expand the capacity of the facility to approximately 30 PF to address the continued increase in demand from DOE/SC researchers; plan for deployment of NERSC-9, which will have three to five times the capacity of NERSC-8, in 2020 to keep pace with growing demand for capacity computing to meet mission needs.

  - **EPA**: Support robust mission-related research program with focus on high-capability computing deployments.

  - **NASA**: Continue development and routine acquisition of HCS resources; incorporate architectures optimized for big data analytics; grow the high-capability computing facility using energy efficient technologies; provide service support across users with diverse requirements through re-compete and award of NACS (NASA Advanced Computing Services) service contract.

  - **NIH**: Support broad-based HCSIA for biomedical computing applications by extending and modernizing HCS facilities and networking on the NIH campus to serve the intramural community.

  - **NOAA**: Provide computational systems to support improved predictive services for weather, climate, and hurricane forecasts. Continue to operate Gaea 1102 Teraflops (TF) Climate Computing HPC (at

DOE's Oak Ridge National Laboratory [DOE/ORNL]); Jet 340 TF Hurricane Forecast Improvement Project (HFIP); allocation on DOE/SC's Titan HPC (roughly equivalent to 500 TF); Theia 1000 TF Sandy Supplemental HPC; expand Theia with another 1000 TF of fine-grained computing; interagency agreement to transfer ownership of Zeus (383 TF) to FBI.

- o **NSF**: Provide world-class computational resources across disciplines to enable major scientific advances. Resources include leadership-class Blue Waters at University of Illinois; ACI Innovation HPC program resources which include Stampede at Texas Advanced Computing Center (TACC), Jetstream (1.2 PF) compute cloud at Indiana University (IU), Bridges (1.2 PF) large memory systems at Pittsburgh Supercomputing Center (PSC), and Comet (2 PF) HPC systems for moderate size jobs at San Diego Supercomputing Center (SDSC); eXtreme Science and Engineering Discovery Environment (XSEDE), which includes high-end visualization and data-analytics systems; other resources include Yellowstone (1.5 PF) system dedicated to the geoscience community at National Center for Atmospheric Research (NCAR), and Wrangler, a 10 PB data resource at TACC.

- **Advancement of HCS applications**

  - o **DoD (HPCMP)**: Mature and demonstrate large and smaller scale software development applications. Multi-physics applications development for acquisition engineering community in air vehicles, ground vehicles, ships, and RF antennas; smaller scale application software development projects to enable the DoD RDT&E community to effectively use next-generation hardware; programming environments, system software, and computational skills transfer for both DoD workforce development and S&T application modernization; Frontier Projects combining multi-million hour allocations with technology transfer and development to advance state-of-the-practice in the application of HPC to the DoD's most challenging problems.

  - o **DOE/SC**: SciDAC partnership to accelerate progress in scientific computing through partnerships among applied mathematicians, computer scientists, and scientists in other disciplines for applications such as climate science, fusion research, high energy physics, nuclear physics, astrophysics, materials science, chemistry, and accelerator physics. Conduct applied mathematics R&D of applied mathematical models, methods, and algorithms for understanding complex natural and engineered systems related to DOE's mission, which underpins all DOE's modeling and simulation efforts and is needed to realize the potential of next-generation HPC systems. Initiate research effort in cybersecurity with emphasis on the unique challenges of DOE's HPC facilities not currently addressed by ongoing cybersecurity R&D.

  - o **EPA**: Develop scientific applications that focus on advanced algorithmic techniques and applied computational/mathematical methods. Develop advanced distributed, massive volume data and modeling capabilities with initial applications to support Air Program goals that focus on air quality models and algorithms, model coupling, and deployment of 3-D application software.

  - o **NASA**: Develop workflow to enable migration to high-capability computing systems; provide data analysis and visualization tools and support that enable exploration of huge datasets; support large-scale M&S and data analysis across NASA's earth and space science, space exploration, and aeronautics research mission areas through High End Computing Capability (HECC) project; support NASA weather and climate modeling simulations and earth science big data research activities through NASA Center for Climate Simulation (NCCS) project.

  - o **NIH**: Harness data and technology to improve health through support of scientific computing efforts such as biomolecular modeling, physiological modeling, and multi-scale modeling that use HCS resources; large scale data management, analytics, and modeling of brain data for the BRAIN Initiative; big data analytics under the Big Data to Knowledge (BD2K) program.

- o **NIST**: Measurement science to speed development and industrial applications of advanced materials; Materials Genome Initiative (development of modeling and simulation techniques, tools; verification and validation, uncertainty quantification [VVUQ]); Advanced Materials Center of Excellence (modeling and informatics to accelerate materials discovery and deployment); measurement infrastructure for high-end computing software (VVUQ); measurement science for visualization (hardware - uncertainty quantification, calibration, and correction; software - uncertainty quantification and visual representation, quantitative methods in visualization); cloud computing standards.

- o **NOAA**: Improve model-based computing of weather and hurricane forecasting and climate prediction.

- o **NSF**: Advance HCS applications broadly, including in areas of national priority, such as the BRAIN (Brain Research through Advancing Innovative Neurotechnologies) Initiative; Advanced Manufacturing Cluster to advance manufacturing and building technologies through predictive and real-time models, novel assembly methods, and control techniques for manufacturing processes; and INFEWS.

- o **OSD**: Advancements in modeling and simulation of challenging environments, algorithm and technology development, and big data applications.

- **High-capability computing systems infrastructure**

- o **DoD (HPCMP)**: Maintain world-class wide-area R&D network to provide access to DoD supercomputing centers - Defense Research and Engineering Network (DREN) at 100 Gbps; cybersecurity operations; frameworks for productivity of non-expert users to enable broader application of HCS-enabled solutions.

- o **DOE/SC**: Small-scale testbed to support a new research effort within the computer science activity for technologies that are "Beyond Moore's Law."

- o **EPA**: Provide infrastructure to combine existing and future data with various temporal and spatial scales, develop and run regional to global models across computational platforms at all scales; archive development and deployment.

- o **NIH**: Continue investment in scientific computing, e.g., software development, neuroscience solicitations, grid computing; National Cancer Institute (NCI) Cancer Genomics Cloud Pilots; develop new shared, interoperable cloud computing environment under BD2K called the "Commons."

- o **NOAA**: Continue to leverage nationwide high-bandwidth, low-latency network to promote cross-agency, shared use of HPC.

- o **NSF**: Provide infrastructure and computational and data capacity to science application activities like UtB, INFEWS, and other application research areas. Infrastructure is also provided by the CIF21, CDS&E, SI^2, DIBBs, and XSEDE programs.

- **Productivity**

- o **DOE/SC and NOAA**: Explore optimal configuration for meta scheduling (Moab).

- o **NOAA**: Explore configuration for job queueing management (Grid).

- o **NASA**: Invest in system and application performance tools that enable full understanding of system and application performance.

- o **NSF**: XMS (XD Metric Services) awarded for development and continued support of XDMoD, a comprehensive HPC system management tool, to further develop it for open source and job-level performance monitoring.

- **Broadening impact**

  - **DoD (HPCMP)**: Develop next-generation computational workforce within DoD via skills development, deployment of both computational and domain-specific expertise to the DoD RDT&E complex, and investments in tools and expertise that match HPC environments to user workflow.

  - **DOE/SC**: Collaborate with other Federal agencies to ensure broad applicability of capable exascale computing across the U.S. Government; in support of NSCI, increase funding to develop next-generation computational science workforce through support of the Computational Science Graduate Fellowship in partnership with DOE/NNSA; continue support for a post-doctoral training program for high end computational science and engineering.

  - **HCSIA agencies**: Continue to advance research and technology in VVUQ; improve user training.

  - **NSF**: Education, training, and outreach activities, led by awards such as XSEDE and Blue Waters, supporting the current and next-generation workforce.

Planning and Coordination Supporting Request

Since 2005, the HCSIA agencies have provided tens of billions of computing hours on the Nation's most powerful computing platforms to enable researchers from academia and industry to address ultra-complex scientific challenges; coordinating this activity remains a major focus of collaboration among the HCSIA agencies and these stakeholders. Another key focus is selecting, evaluating, procuring, and operating Federal high-end platforms – a complicated, labor-intensive process that the HCSIA agencies work closely together to streamline. A third major focus of collaborative activities is development of sharable computational approaches for investigation and analysis across the sciences. Cooperative activities under each of the HCSIA strategic priorities include:

- **Leadership-class and production HCS systems**

  - **Leadership-class and production computing**: Coordination to make highest capability HCS resources available to the broad research community and industry – DoD (HPCMP), DOE/SC, NASA, NIST, NOAA, and NSF

  - **DOE interagency collaboration**: Multiagency review of the DOE/NNSA and DOE/SC preliminary plan for the Exascale Computing Initiative (ECI) – DoD (HPCMP), NASA, NIH, NOAA, NSA, and NSF

  - **DOE intra-agency collaborations**: Joint system procurements for next advanced technology systems delivered in 2017 and co-design for future systems – DOE/NNSA and DOE/SC

- **Advancement of HCS applications**

  - **DOE intra-agency collaborations**: SciDAC-3 institutes and partnerships continue – DOE/NNSA and DOE/SC

  - **DOE/SC computing facilities**: Provide over 11 billion core hours in 2015. NERSC – 2.575 billion core hours; OLCF – 3.350 billion core hours; ALCF – 5.150 billion core hours

  - **Multi-scale modeling in biomedical, biological, and behavioral systems**: Interagency collaboration to advance modeling of complex living systems – DoD, NIH, and NSF

  - **Leadership computing**: Allocate hours for projects such as climate, weather, and water model runs – DOE/SC and NOAA, and study of flow of suspensions – DOE/SC and NIST

  - **XSEDE, Petascale Computing Resource Allocations (PRAC)**: Provide 4-5 billion core compute hours to the open science community, spanning research of multiple agencies; all disciplines represented – HEC IWG agencies and other agencies

- o **Computational toxicology**: Integration of HCS technologies with molecular biology to improve methods for risk assessment of chemicals – DoD, DOE/SC, FDA, and NIH

- o **Earth System Modeling Framework (ESMF) and Earth Systems Grid Federation (ESGF)**: DoD, DOE/SC, NASA, NOAA, and NSF

- o **High-resolution Alaska Digital Elevation Model (DEM) production**: DOE, NASA, NGA, and NSF

- o **Simulation study of cement hydration**: NIST and NSF

- **High-capability computing systems infrastructure**

  - o **Remote Sensing Information Gateway (RSIG)**: Allows users to integrate their selected environmental datasets into a unified visualization – DOE/SC, EPA, NASA, and NOAA

  - o **Computational research infrastructure (CC*DNI, IRNC, ESnet, N-Wave, Hawaii and Alaska connectivity)**: Provide networking to support U.S. and international research communities for access to and between high-capability computing resources supporting networking research, large-scale data flows, end-to-end throughput, real-time networking, and applications – DOE/SC, DREN, NASA, NOAA, and NSF

  Budget for computational research infrastructure is reported under the HCSIA PCA, but coordination is through the LSN CG. The LSN CG coordinates that portion of HCSIA that entails large-scale networking infrastructure in support of high-capability computing.

- **Productivity**

  - o **System reviews, benchmarking, metrics**: Collaborations – DoD (HPCMP), DOE/NNSA, DOE/SC, NASA, NOAA, NSA, and NSF

  - o **DOE HPC operations review**: Share processes and practices for delivering facilities and services that enable high performance data-driven scientific discovery – DOE/NNSA and DOE/SC, with participation from multiple agencies

- **Broadening impact**

  - o **Interagency participation in proposal review panels, principal investigator meetings** – HEC IWG agencies

  - o **Extending awareness**: Explore ways to increase awareness of the importance of U.S. leadership in HCS – HEC IWG agencies

  - o **Explore ways to maximize HCS resources for compute and data allocations** – HEC IWG agencies

  - o **Strategic planning**: Participate in strategic initiatives to maintain U.S. leadership in HCS – HEC IWG agencies

  - o **Education/workforce development**: Support a Federal HCS inventory portal for learning and workforce development resources – HEC IWG agencies

  - o **Metrics**: Explore alternatives to Linpack benchmark to establish more meaningful measures for performance of U.S. HCS systems – HEC IWG agencies

  - o **Green computing**: Promote energy-efficient "green" computing practices and explore methods to dramatically reduce HCS energy consumption and related energy costs – DoD (HPCMP), DOE/SC, and NASA

  - o **Technology transfer**: Transfer of computational skills and technologies to partners in industry and academia – HEC IWG agencies

- **NSCI**: Coordinate with other agencies on initiatives to maintain and enhance U.S. leadership in HCS – HEC IWG and other agencies

Additional 2016 and 2017 Activities by Agency

The following list provides a summary of individual agencies' ongoing programmatic interests for 2016 and 2017 under the HCSIA PCA:

- **DoD (HPCMP)**: The Computational Research Engineering Acquisition Tools and Environments (CREATE) initiative demonstrates and matures advanced application codes to allow scientists and engineers to use supercomputers to design and analyze virtual prototypes of DoD ships, fixed-wing aircraft, rotorcraft, ground vehicles, and radio frequency (RF) antennas; Frontier projects represent and support the DoD's highest-priority, highest-impact computational work, both from a technical and mission-relevance standpoint.

- **DOE/SC**: Operate Hopper (1.3 PF) and Edison (2.4 PF) systems at LBNL, the Mira (10 PF) system at ANL, and the Titan (27 PF) system at ORNL. Exascale requirements reviews – Offices of Advanced Scientific Computing Research (ASCR) and Basic Energy Sciences (BES) in November 2015; ASCR and Fusion Energy Sciences (FES) in January 2016.

- **DOE and NSF**: Provide support for Open Science Grid (OSG) services and resources to integrate campus resources for high throughput computing.

- **NASA**: High-capability computing center facility study with focus on options to grow the computing center within the current budget constraints; explore hybrid cloud-computing capability in HCS environment, focusing on big data applications.

- **NIH**: Fund predominantly broad-based biocomputing awards.

- **NIST**: Parallel and distributed algorithms and tools for measurement science, including fundamental mathematical tool, uncertainty quantification, image analysis, materials science, and virtual measurement laboratory.

- **NOAA**: Investments in applied research projects in the areas of adoption of advanced computing, communications, and information technology.

- **NSF**: Provide advanced compute, data, and visualization resources from campus-level to leadership-class; enhance productivity and broaden participation (XSEDE).

- **OSD**: Incorporate Electromagnetic Spectrum (EMS) object models and target folder utilizing cloud-based data processing; autonomous systems for daily military operations, including force protection and special operations.

High Confidence Software and Systems (HCSS)

NITRD Agencies: DARPA, DHS, DoD Service Research Organizations, DOE, NASA, NIH, NIST, NOAA, NSA, NSF, and OSD
Other Participants: DOT, FAA, FDA, FHWA, NRC, and USDA/NIFA

HCSS R&D supports development of scientific foundations and innovative and enabling software and hardware technologies for the engineering, verification and validation, assurance, standardization, and certification of complex, networked, distributed computing systems and cyber-physical (IT-enabled) systems (CPS). The goal is to enable seamless, fully synergistic integration of computational intelligence, communication, control, sensing, actuation, and adaptation with physical devices and information processes to routinely realize high-confidence, optimally performing systems that are essential for effectively operating life-, safety-, security-, and mission-critical applications. These systems must be capable of interacting correctly, safely, and securely with humans and the physical world in changing environments and unforeseen conditions. In many cases, they must be certifiable. In some cases, dependability and trustworthy interaction with humans or other CPSs are sufficient. The vision is to realize dependable systems that are precise and highly efficient; respond quickly; work in dangerous or inaccessible environments; provide large-scale, distributed coordination; augment human capabilities; and enhance societal quality of life. New science and technology are needed to build these systems with computing, communication, information, and control pervasively embedded at all levels, thus enabling entirely new generations of engineering designs that can enhance U.S. competitiveness across economic and industrial sectors.

HCSS Coordination: For the HCSS PCA, agencies coordinate their R&D activities through the High Confidence Software and Systems Coordinating Group (HCSS CG) and the Cyber Physical Systems Senior Steering Group (CPS SSG). Agencies may also coordinate through a new NITRD group (to be named) on crosscutting topics or activities in robotics and intelligent systems (RIS PCA). For clarity, the association of a particular NITRD group with a particular coordination activity that crosscuts PCAs is provided below, as needed.

President's FY 2017 Request

Strategic Priorities Underlying This Request

In recent years, the HCSS agencies have engaged in a sustained effort to foster a new multidisciplinary research agenda that will enable the United States to lead in the development of next-generation engineered systems that depend on ubiquitous cyber control and require very high levels of system assurance. Through a variety of ongoing activities, the HCSS effort is forging a nationwide community interested in the CPS research challenges faced in common across such economic sectors as medicine and healthcare, energy, transportation, manufacturing, and agriculture, and across such agency missions as national security, environmental protection, and space exploration. The HCSS agencies have set the following priorities for research coordination:

- **Science and technology for building cyber-physical systems**: Develop a new systems science providing unified foundations, models and tools, system capabilities, and architectures that enable innovation in highly dependable cyber-enabled engineered and natural systems; develop public domain, cyber-physical testbeds.

- **Management of complex and autonomous systems**: Develop measurement and understanding for improved models of complex systems of systems, shared control and authority, levels of autonomy, human-system interactions, and integrated analytical and decision-support tools; integrate computer and information-centric physical and engineered systems.

- **Assurance technology**: Develop a sound scientific and technological basis, including formal methods and computational frameworks, for assured design, construction, analysis, evaluation, and implementation of reliable, robust, safe, secure, stable, and certifiably dependable systems regardless of size, scale, complexity, and heterogeneity; develop software and system-engineering tool capabilities to achieve application and problem domain-based assurance, and broadly embed these capabilities within the system engineering process; reduce the effort, time, and cost of assurance ("affordable" verification and validation [V&V]/certification) – such methods will need to preserve safety yet dramatically reduce the "test space" when it comes to manned, unmanned, and mixed authority systems spanning a variety of disciplines; provide a technology base of advanced-prototype implementations of high-confidence technologies to spur adoption; design and install resilient energy delivery systems capable of surviving a cyber-incident while sustaining critical functions; support development of regulations and guidance for assurance of safety and security.

- **High-confidence real-time software and systems**: Pursue innovative design, development, and engineering approaches to ensure the dependability, safety, security, performance, and evolution of software-intensive, dynamic, networked control systems in life- and safety-critical infrastructure domains, including systems-of-systems environments; real-time embedded applications and systems software; component-based accelerated design and verifiable system integration; predictable, fault-tolerant, distributed software and systems; modeling of heterogeneous distributed systems using unified mathematical framework; develop safety assurance tools and techniques to build justifiable confidence in aerospace and national airspace systems; develop infrastructure for medical device integration and interoperability, patient modeling and simulation, and adaptive patient-specific algorithms.

- **Translation into mission-oriented research**: Leverage multiagency research to move theory into practice, using challenges and competitions, for example, to solve problems in domains such as energy, cyber-physical ground and air transportation systems, and connected vehicle-to-infrastructure systems.

- **CPS education**: Launch an initiative to integrate CPS theory and methodology into education and promote increased understanding of and interest in CPS through the development of new curricula at all levels that engage both the physical and cyber disciplines and foster a new generation of U.S. experts.

- **Secure, dependable Internet of Things (IoT)**: Develop foundational theory and methods that enable IoT devices and systems to operate securely and dependably in interactions with other systems and humans.

Highlights of the Request

The HCSS agencies report the following topical areas as highlights of their planned R&D investments for FY 2017. Agencies are listed in alphabetical order:

- **Cyber-physical systems**: Explore the fundamental scientific, engineering, and technological principles that underpin the integration of cyber and physical elements, making the "systems you can bet your life on" possible; continue support for research to enable physical, biological, and engineered systems whose operations are integrated, monitored, and/or controlled by a computational core and interact with the physical world, with components networked at every scale and computing deeply embedded in every physical component, possibly even in materials; real-time embedded, distributed systems and software; CEMMSS to model and simulate systems interdependent with the physical world and social systems; safety models and designs for cyber-physical medical systems, including interoperable ("plug-and-play") medical devices. – DoD Service research organizations, FDA, NASA, NIH, NIST, NSA, NSF, OSD, and VA

- **Complex systems**: Multiyear effort, including focus on software for tomorrow's complex systems such as CPS, to address challenges of interacting systems of systems, including human-system interactions, and investigate their non-linear interactions and aggregate or emergent phenomena to better predict system capabilities and decision-making about complex systems; develop new algorithms for functional analysis of real-time software, control effects of multicore memory access on CPS real-time behavior, and flexible and predictable control of multiple, semi-autonomous Unmanned Aerial Vehicles (UAVs); joint capability technology demonstration of flexible mission-reprogramming, increased endurance, and increased autonomy. – AFRL, FAA, FHWA, NASA, NIH, NIST, NSF, and OSD

- **High-confidence systems and foundations of assured computing**: Formal methods and tools for modeling, designing, measuring, analyzing, evaluating, and predicting performance, correctness, efficiency, dependability, scalability, safety, security, and usability of complex, real-time, distributed, and mobile software and systems; high-assurance environments from COTs; high-assurance virtualization and measurement; architectures, components, composition, and configuration; engineering, analysis, and testing of software and hardware; architecture, tools, and competence for assurance certifiable safe systems; cost-effective V&V; verification techniques for separation assurance algorithms; safety cases, standards, and metrics; quantum information processing. – AFOSR, AFRL, ARO, FDA, NASA, NIH, NIST, NSA, NSF, ONR, and OSD

- **Information assurance requirements**: Methods and tools for constructing, analyzing security structures (management architectures and protocols, etc.); assurance technologies for cross-domain creation, editing, sharing of sensitive information in collaboration environments that span multiple security levels; cryptographic algorithms and engineering; assured compilation of cryptographic designs, specifications to platforms of interest - NSA and ONR; testing infrastructure for health IT standards, specifications, certification (with HHS); cross-enterprise document sharing in electronic health systems; standards and quality measurement systems for smart manufacturing, measurement science and standards for CPS engineering; build a testbed to help industry, university, and government collaborators develop an open standards platform to facilitate the simultaneous engineering of the physical and virtual components of manufacturing systems. – NIH, NIST, and NSF

- **Aviation safety**: R&D in transformative V&V methods to rigorously assure the safety of aviation systems. This includes considerations for all classes of aircraft and anticipated future air traffic management capabilities. Develop and demonstrate innovative technologies in the design of architectures with advanced features, focusing on designing for high-confidence, standardization, and certification. – AFRL, FAA, NASA, and OSD

- **Assurance of Flight-Critical Systems (AFCS)**: Provide appropriate airworthiness requirements for Unmanned Aircraft Systems (UAS) that help enable routine access to the National Airspace System (NAS); enable assurance that new technologies envisioned for the Next Generation Air Transportation System (NextGen) are as safe as, or safer than, the current system and provide a cost-effective basis for assurance and certification of complex civil aviation systems; develop and analyze formal models of air traffic management systems for safety properties incorporating the effects of uncertainty. – AFRL, FAA, and NASA

Planning and Coordination Supporting Request

To build multidisciplinary communities of interest both within and across sectors, the HCSS agencies annually hold workshops and other research meetings that bring a broad mix of stakeholders together. These gatherings help forge a wider understanding of critical issues and develop consensus around promising research directions in high-confidence CPS. At its regular meetings, the HCSS CG also gives each agency the opportunity to share information about its budget priorities, technologies, challenges, and successes in HCSS. The following are ongoing HCSS coordination activities:

- **National Research Workshop Series**: Academic, industry, and government stakeholder workshops to identify new R&D for building 21st century CPS for life-, safety-, and mission-critical applications. Topics for FY 2017 include:

  o **National Workshop on Transportation Cyber-Physical Systems** – AFRL, DOT, FAA, FDA, FHWA, NASA, NIST, NSA, and NSF

- o **Cyber-manufacturing**: Workshop to focus on issues at the nexus of computer science and manufacturing – NSF with other HCSS agencies

- o **Smart and Connected Communities**: Multiple workshops in the early planning stages – NSF with other HCSS agencies

- **CPS Week:** Annual High Confidence Networked Systems (HiCoNS) meeting – AFRL, DHS, NASA, NIST, NSA, and NSF

- **Static Analysis Tools Exposition (SATE)**: Annual summit on software security for vendors, users, and academics – NIST, NSA, and NSF in collaboration with DHS

- **CPS Education**: NSA, NSF, and ONR

- **Scholar-In-Residence Program at FDA** – FDA and NSF

- **Software Assurance Metrics and Tool Evaluation**: Annual workshop for users and developers to compare efficacy of techniques and tools; develop vulnerability taxonomies – DHS, NIST, and NSA

- **Safe and Secure Software and Systems Symposium (S5)**: Industry, academia, and government collaborate on improving the airworthiness and assurance certification process of future aerospace flight control systems with both incremental and revolutionary technological innovations in safety and security V&V techniques that support maintaining cost and risk at acceptable levels – AFRL, NASA, NSA, and NSF

- **Annual HCSS Conference**: Showcasing of promising research to improve system confidence – DARPA, FAA, NASA, NSA with NSF, ONR, and OSD

- **Software Assurance Forum**: Coordinate software certification initiatives and activities for Systems containing Software (ScS) – DHS, DoD Service research organizations, NIST, NSA, and OSD

- **Safety of flight-critical systems**: Workshops and technical discussion – AFRL, NASA, NSA, and NSF

- **Standards, software assurance metrics for Supervisory Control and Data Acquisition (SCADA), Industrial Control Systems (ICS)**: Collaborative development – NIST and others

- **Biomedical imagery**: Technical standards for change measurements in patient applications – FDA, NIH, and NIST

- **Cooperative proposal evaluation** – AFRL, FAA, FDA, NASA, NIST, NRC, NSA, NSF, and OSD

- **FAA National Software and Airborne Electronic Hardware Standardization Conference** – FAA, NASA, and OSD

- **NASA Formal Methods Symposium (NFM 2016)** – AFRL, FAA, FDA, NASA, NIST, NSF, NSA, and OSD

- **Connected vehicle R&D**: Connected vehicle testbeds, connected vehicle pilot deployments, human factors for shared control, and vehicle to infrastructure systems – DOT, FHWA, NIST, and NSF

- **National Robotics Initiative (NRI)**: Cross-cutting program to accelerate the development and use of robots that work beside, or cooperatively with, people – DoD, DOE/EM, NASA, NIH, NSF, and USDA/NIFA

Budget for the NRI is reported under the RIS PCA, but the HCSS CG coordinates that portion of RIS that entails the safe, dependable operation of robots developed and used cooperatively with people.

Additional 2016 and 2017 Activities by Agency

The following list provides a summary of individual agencies' ongoing programmatic interests for 2016 and 2017 under the HCSS PCA:

- **AFRL**: Research is driven by the strategic goals of the "Autonomy Community of Interest (COI), Test and Evaluation, Verification and Validation (TEVV) Investment Strategy 2015-2018," released June 2015.[9] Goals include: 1) Methods and Tools Assisting in Requirements Development and Analysis, 2) Evidence-Based Design and Implementation, 3) Cumulative Evidence through Research, Developmental, and Operational Testing, 4) Run Time Behavior Prediction and Recovery, and 5) Assurance Arguments for Autonomous Systems. As a result of the strategy, the Test Resource Management Center (TRMC) - Unmanned Autonomous Systems Test (UAST) group is investigating how to change the Test and Evaluation (T&E) infrastructure to accommodate future autonomous systems. Additionally, AFRL in partnership with the OSD Scientific Test and Analysis Techniques in Test & Evaluation Center of Excellence (STAT in T&E COE) investigated research into changing the current T&E processes and methods for autonomous systems. Finally, AFRL led an OSD-funded seedling effort to investigate licensure-based certification of autonomy. This study is investigating a separate TEVV model for autonomous agents, which is similar to a licensure model for human operators, and how an autonomous agent might be designed to accommodate such an approach.

- **FAA**: Improve and maintain methods for approving digital systems for aircraft and air traffic control (ATC) systems and prepare for the Next Generation Air Transportation System (NextGen) by conducting research in advanced digital (software-based and airborne electronic hardware [AEH]-based airborne systems) technology; keep abreast of and adapt to the rapid, frequent changes and increasing complexity in aircraft and ATC systems; understand and assess safe implementations in flight-essential and flight-critical systems (e.g., fly-by-wire flight controls, navigation and communication equipment, autopilots, and other aircraft and engine functions); and continue work on digital requirements for software-development techniques and tools, airborne electronic hardware design techniques and tools, onboard network security and integrity, and system considerations for complex digitally intensive systems.

- **FDA**: Provide means and methods (assured verification) for establishing the integrity of medical devices that scale from cellular compositions to large radiation therapy systems, discrete (external and implantable) unit platforms to distributed, mobile, remote, system of systems, and robotics and robotics-assisted architectures. Research includes formal methods model-based device design, software and system safety, security, human computer interaction modeling and certification, component composition analysis, forensics analysis, engineering tool foundations, metrics for quality, patient physiological modeling, adaptive patient-specific algorithms, and physiological human in-the-loop control systems.

- **FHWA**: Apply concepts from fundamental advances in CPS science for a new transportation paradigm of connected highway and vehicle systems in support of broad mission goals: making traffic deaths or serious injuries rare events, optimizing mobility so that personal travel and goods movement are easy and reliable within, between, and across modal systems, and reducing the energy and resources required for highway transportation in the United States. Spur research that intertwines automated control systems with health monitoring sensors for highway transportation structures and pavements to create true, fully functioning cyber-physical systems that will ensure a state of good repair for the Nation's roads and respond to both every day and extreme environmental changes.

- **NASA**: Perform R&D activities to enable high confidence in aviation systems supporting safe, efficient growth in global operations; real-time, system-wide safety assurance; and assured autonomy for aviation

---

[9] "DoD Autonomy COI Test and Evaluation, Verification and Validation (TEVV) Investment Strategy 2015-2018," Assistant Secretary of Defense / Research and Engineering (ASD/R&E), Autonomy Community of Interest (COI), June 2015: http://www.defenseinnovationmarketplace.mil/resources/OSD_ATEVV_STRAT_DIST_A_SIGNED.pdf .

transformation. Specific activities include: maturation of assurance case techniques for use on complex aviation systems; advancing formal methods techniques for assuring complex software-intensive systems; advancing assurance technologies to enable deployment of UAS in the NAS; and design and analysis of operational procedures, algorithms and enabling technologies for air traffic control.

- **NIH**: Translational research in biomedical technology to enhance development, testing, and implementation of diagnostics and therapeutics that require advanced CPS innovations; assurance in medical devices such as pulse oximeters and infusion pumps, cardio-exploratory monitors for neonates; telemedicine; computer-aided detection and diagnosis; computer-aided surgery and treatment; neural interface technologies such as cochlear implants, and brain-computer interfaces. Systematic exploration of the sources and variability introduced during tumor image acquisition and tumor size measurement, for the development of improved algorithms used in assessment of new therapies; and development of new data acquisition and analysis methods to aid in the determination of optimal ultrasound exposure settings to obtain the necessary diagnostic information by using the very lowest total energy for increased patient safety

- **NIST**: Conduct measurement science research and make critical technical contributions to standards that advance High Confidence Software and Systems. Key programmatic activities include the Cyber-Physical Systems Public Working Group, the Global City Teams Challenge, and development of a CPS testbed to advance measurement science and standards enabling CPS development and deployment. Additional projects and activities include Cybersecurity for Smart Manufacturing Systems (part of the NIST Smart Manufacturing Operations Planning and Control program) to help secure industrial control systems used in manufacturing and CPS; Software Assurance Metrics and Tool Evaluation (SAMATE – with DHS funding) and Software Assurance Reference Dataset (SARD) to help provide confidence that software is free from vulnerabilities; National Vulnerability Database; Security Content Automation Protocol (SCAP); and Internet infrastructure protection (with DHS funding). Related research topic areas include seamless mobility; trustworthy information systems; information security automation, combinatorial testing; next-generation access control; and smart manufacturing.

- **NRC**: Regulatory research to aid safety and security in cyber-physical systems (digital instrumentation and control systems) used in the nuclear energy sector.

- **NSA**: High-assurance system design (correct-by-construction methods, model-driven development, programming languages) and analysis (concolic execution, multi-tool analysis, separation/matching logic, static/dynamic analysis), with focus on usability; assured implementation, execution of critical platform components and functionality; and assured cryptographic implementations (software and hardware); domain-specific workbench developments (cryptography, guards, protocols).

- **NSF**: Address HCSS research challenges through the multi-directorate Cyber Physical Systems (CPS) and National Robotics Initiative (NRI) programs that focus on foundational research in designing safe, secure, and resilient systems operating in uncertain and dynamic environments. CPS program: foundations; methods and tools; and components, run-time substrates, and systems. Continue major research thrust in methods for system verification including manned, unmanned, and mixed authority systems, with a focus on methods that can preserve safety properties yet also enable rapid and affordable verification of complex systems including transportation (air, ground, space, and sea), healthcare, energy, and manufacturing domains. CPS also addresses foundational research needed to harness the power of the Internet of Things (IoT) and achieve the Internet of Dependable and Controllable Things at enormous scale. NRI program: accelerate the development and use of robotics cooperatively with people including operation that must be safe and dependable. Cyber-manufacturing: Coordinate the FY 2015 Cyber-manufacturing solicitation that requested proposals for small, innovative projects to investigate the interfaces among distributed design, the machine translation of part descriptions into manufacturing instructions, and networked manufacturing resources. The activities emphasize university-based testbeds and integration of classroom and laboratory-based work and workshops. These activities are expected to continue in FY 2016 and into FY 2017.

- **OSD**: Improve the DoD's ability to design, build, test, and sustain software-intensive cyber-physical systems that meet DoD mission-critical requirements for embedded and distributed systems, exhibit predictable behavior, and enable affordable evolution and interoperability; includes specification of complex requirements; "correct-by-construction" software development; scalable composition; high-confidence software and middleware; system architectures for network-centric environments; technologies for system visualization, testing, verification, and validation; model- and platform-based design and development approaches; and tools for controlling automated exploration and evaluation of massive trade spaces.

Human Computer Interaction and Information Management (HCI&IM)

NITRD Agencies: AHRQ, DHS, DoD Service Research Organizations, EPA, NARA, NIH, NIST, NASA, NOAA, and NSF

HCI&IM focuses on R&D to expand human capabilities through collaboration and communication technologies and information management. Expanding human capabilities requires R&D in visualization, collaborative systems, multimodal system engagements, and human cognition—including perception, intuition, learning, cognitive load, and problem solving for human-in-the-loop systems. HCI&IM research covers data collection and interaction with datasets that are critical to national priorities, such as defense, energy, the environment, and healthcare. HCI&IM research also enables advancements in public access to data, modeling and simulation, informatics, and technologies that support a broad innovation enterprise across science and engineering.

HCI&IM research focuses on the technologies that improve how people access and use digital information by expanding the capabilities of computing systems and devices to process data and make information accessible. Transformative approaches for accessing, interacting with, and displaying data are critical to advancing human capabilities in understanding and deriving meaning from data. The Federal Government generates and maintains the world's largest digital collections of science and engineering data, records, health information, and scientific and other types of archival literature. Discovering knowledge from these data and from the vast sources of distributed, heterogeneous, and streaming data that are created every day requires new methods, tools, technologies, and ways to integrate humans in the discovery process. These capabilities are essential for the technological innovations that fuel and grow the U.S. economy.

> **HCI&IM Coordination**: For the HCI&IM PCA, agencies coordinate their R&D activities through the Human Computer Interaction and Information Management Coordinating Group (HCI&IM CG). Agencies may also coordinate through a new NITRD group (to be named) on crosscutting topics or activities in robotics and intelligent systems (RIS PCA). For clarity, the association of a particular NITRD group with a particular coordination activity that crosscuts PCAs is provided below, as needed.

President's FY 2017 Request

Strategic Priorities Underlying This Request

Strategic priorities in HCI&IM include:

- **Data quality, access, sharing, and validation:** Multiagency coordination that allows for data sharing while assuring users of the quality and provenance of the data.

- **Scientific visualization:** Visualization, including modeling and simulation, is essential to the development of effective decision-making technologies, anomaly detection, and the tailoring of individual and collaborative work spaces that reflect individual differences in cognitive processing and perception.

- **Information integration:**

  - **Information management systems** enable individuals and organizations to create, share, and apply information to gain value and achieve specific objectives and priorities.

  - **Standards** provide a way to ensure effective human system interaction and establish the basis for interoperability essential to integrating and managing data.

Highlights of the Request

The HCI&IM agencies report the following areas as highlights of their planned R&D investments for FY 2017. Agencies are listed in alphabetical order:

- **Transforming data to knowledge**: New computing research in modeling and simulation, algorithms, and tools is necessary to accelerate scientific discovery and productivity from heterogeneous data stores, and development of innovative, multidimensional methods for processing highly complex data. New ways should be developed to enable the intuitive display of complex interactions and mechanisms that enhance both discovery and use of data. – AHRQ, DoD Service research organizations, EPA, NARA, NASA, NIH, NIST, NOAA, NSF, and other agencies

- **Human engagement and decision-making**: Research to design effective HCI and systems integration to optimize human capabilities requires human-performance modeling, multimodal interfaces, and mechanisms for distributed collaboration, knowledge management, virtual organizations, and visual environments. This has a crosslink to cognitive and perceptual process modeling and measurement. Expansion of virtual reality technologies is necessary for simulation and training. Usability research is critical for the improvement of biometric and voting systems. – DoD Service research organizations, EPA, NASA, NIST, NOAA, and NSF

- **Effective stewardship of science and engineering data**: This effort will maximize the value gained from current and previous Federal investments but will require additional research in providing for life-cycle stewardship over time. Research foci include personalized access to information, as well as federation, preservation, and analysis of large, heterogeneous collections of scientific data, information, and records. A persistent issue is the need for fault-tolerant, scalable management of information input and output in light of new system architectures. – EPA, NARA, NASA, NIH, NIST, NOAA, NSF, and other agencies

- **Information integration, accessibility, and management**: Multiple advances are required in technologies, system architectures, and tools for optimized, scalable ingest and processing for high-capacity data integration (especially of Geographic Information System [GIS] and spatio-temporal data), management, exploitation, modeling, and analysis. Research continues in cloud-based infrastructures to efficiently gain distributed access to data resources utilizing new ontologies and metadata formats for discovery. – AHRQ, EPA, NARA, NASA, NIH, NIST, NOAA, and NSF

- **Earth/space science data and information systems**: These efforts enable multiagency access to and use of Federal scientific data resources through Web-based tools and services (e.g., remote visualization) that exploit advances in computer science and technology. – EPA, NASA, NOAA, NSF, and other agencies

- **Health information technologies**: NITRD's Health IT R&D Community of Practice is developing guidance for R&D in this area. Research needs that have been identified include expansion of clinical decision-support systems, development of more effective use of electronic health records and data, and defining national health information and device interoperability standards. – AHRQ, FDA, NIH, NIST, NSF, ONC, and other agencies

- **Information search and retrieval**: New research methods and tools are necessary for evaluation and performance measures of information-discovery technologies, as well as relevance feedback. Current focus areas include legal discovery, recognition of opinion, and patent search, as well as domain-specific search and machine reading of records. – NARA, NIST, and NSF

- **Cognitive, adaptive, and intelligent systems**: Algorithmic and multidisciplinary research is designed to discover the cognitive, perceptual modeling for joint cognitive systems design; autonomy, trustworthiness, and reliability of automated systems; engineered intelligence and adaptability; robotics, human-robot teaming; automated computational intelligence; affective computing. – DoD Service research organizations, NARA, NASA, NIST, and NSF

Budget for robotics and intelligent systems are reported under the RIS PCA, but coordination of these aspects of RIS is through the HCI&IM CG.

- **Multimodal language recognition and translation**: Improve multilingual language technology performance in areas of speech-to-text transcription and text-to-text transcription. A goal is to provide spontaneous two-way communications translation, machine reading, text retrieval, document summarization/distillation, automatic content extraction, and speaker and language recognition through multimodal interfaces. – DoD Service research organizations, NARA, NASA, NIST, and NSF

Planning and Coordination Supporting Request

Although the HCI&IM portfolio includes a broad range of enabling technologies, the current focus of coordination among the agencies is the overriding challenge of ultra-scale, heterogeneous data: how to manage it, enable interoperability and usability, and develop new infrastructures and tools that broaden access and exploration to a wider range of end users. The following HCI&IM collaborations seek to forward this agenda:

- **Foundations of visualization and analysis**: This provides a multiagency mechanism for coordination of research in feature extraction for anomaly detection, integration of multiple types of data and records, the use of visualization as an interface, and biomedical imaging. The follow-on activities in the "Frontiers of Visualization" meeting series will focus on research needs in various knowledge areas. – AHRQ, EPA, NARA, NASA, NIH, NIST, NOAA, NSF, and other agencies

- **Biodiversity and Ecosystem Informatics Working Group**: The group provides an ongoing Federal point of contact and body for cooperation, with a focus on aspects of the environment, natural resources, and sustainability as outlined in the July 2011 PCAST report *Sustaining Environmental Capital: Protecting Society and the Economy.*[10] – DoD, DOE/SC, EPA, Interior, NASA, NIH, NOAA, NSF, and other agencies

- **Earth/space science, climate, and weather**: Agencies focus on cooperative activities in providing interoperable data (including through the Big Earth Data Initiative), multidimensional models, and tools for better understanding and prediction based on the growing corpus of observational and experimental data. – DoD Service research organizations, EPA, NASA, NOAA, NSF, and other agencies

- **Information access, management, and preservation**: Multiple agencies work together to meet Administration requirements in data and publications access. Agencies have also been called to meet requirements identified in the Presidential Records Management Directive[11] focusing on electronic recordkeeping. This includes a requirement to manage all email in electronic form by December 31, 2016. – DOE, EPA, NARA, NASA, NIH, NIST, NOAA, NSF, and other agencies

- **Usability**: People are the ultimate users of information. Usability research draws input from the social and behavioral sciences and informs the design and evaluation of technical solutions with the goal of ease of use. Research areas include health IT, security, voting, biometrics systems, and decision-support systems. – AHRQ, NIST, and NSF

---

[10] *Sustaining Environmental Capital: Protecting Society and the Economy.* July 2011, PCAST: http://www.whitehouse.gov/sites/default/files/microsites/ostp/pcast_sustaining_environmental_capital_report.pdf.

[11] OMB-NARA Memorandum on Managing Government Records Directive (M-12-18), August 24, 2012: https://www.whitehouse.gov/sites/default/files/omb/memoranda/2012/m-12-18.pdf.

Additional 2016 and 2017 Activities by Agency

The following list provides a summary of individual agencies' ongoing programmatic interests for 2016 and 2017 under the HCI&IM PCA:

- **AFRL**: Research and technologies to enhance the decision making of Remotely Piloted Aircraft (RPA) operators, Intelligence, Surveillance, and Reconnaissance (ISR) analysts, and Command and Control (C2) personnel. This will include new visual analytic, mathematical, structured data analysis, representational, and transformation methods; perceptual and cognitive models to support advanced visualizations, work aids, and multi-modal interaction design; and advanced displays for fusion of sensor and intelligence information. The results will be improved situation awareness and enhanced time-critical comprehension of complex, probabilistic, and multi-domain spatial and temporal data.

- **AHRQ**: Quality measurement and improvement; healthcare decision making; patient and clinician information needs; U.S. Health Information Knowledgebase; evidence-based practice center reports.

- **EPA**: Databases for computational toxicology; scientific information management (tools, best practices for management, accessibility of complex EPA datasets); distributed environmental applications and advanced cross-platform visualizations.

- **NARA**: Global-scale, open source, next-generation technologies, architectures, and services enabling effective, sustainable management, intellectual control, and access to nationally distributed billion-file-and-larger scale, complex digital object collections.

- **NIH**: Collaborative Research in Computational Neuroscience (CRCNS) - Innovative Approaches to Science and Engineering Research on Brain Function; Big Data Centers of Excellence; Analysis of Genome-Wide Gene-Environment (GxE) Interactions; focus areas include decision making for patients and clinicians, natural language understanding, organization and retrieval of health-related information by consumers, visualization and mapping of heterogeneous data for clinical researchers, support for healthy behaviors, and device interfaces.

- **NIST**: Biometrics evaluation, usability, and standards (fingerprint, face, iris, voice/speaker); multimedia measurement and evaluation methods (video retrieval, audio and video analysis); data preservation and data science metrology; multimodal analytics; usability and user-centered research for cybersecurity infrastructure, health information technology, cloud computing, voting systems, public safety communication, and privacy; mathematical knowledge management.

- **NOAA**: Technologies for real-time weather/climate data in multiple formats for scientists, forecasters, first responders, and citizens; remote visualization via N-Wave, new high-definition devices; disaster planning, mitigation, response, and recovery.

- **NSF**: Through academic R&D, NSF supports CIF21 as well as programs in support of information privacy, data and open publication access, ubiquitous networked data environments, human-computer partnerships, socially intelligent computing, understanding the science of information, cognition mechanisms in human learning, and remote access to experimental facilities.

Large-Scale Data Management and Analysis (LSDMA)

NITRD Agencies: DARPA, DHS, DOE/NNSA, DOE/SC, EPA, NARA, NASA, NIH, NIST, NOAA, NSA, NSF, and OSD
Other Participants: USAID and USGS

LSDMA focuses on R&D to improve the management and analysis of large-scale data in order to extract knowledge and insight from large, diverse, and disparate sources of data, including the mechanisms for data capture, curation, management, and access.

LSDMA research focuses on next-generation methods, technologies, and tools that are capable of integrating and efficiently managing large-scale streaming, distributed, and heterogeneous information sources. Research will enable advancements in data management and analysis, knowledge discovery, and insights that lead to confident action. Progress requires the development of clearly defined ethical practices to protect data privacy and improve security, a competent workforce, and opportunities for partnerships and collaborations.

> **LSDMA Coordination**: For the LSDMA PCA, agencies coordinate their R&D activities through the Big Data Senior Steering Group (BD SSG).

President's FY 2017 Request

Strategic Priorities Underlying This Request

Strategic priorities in LSDMA include:

- **Next-generation capabilities**: To leverage emerging large-scale data techniques, and technologies, research next-generation capabilities that apply to agency missions and will help drive the Nation's economy.

- **Trustworthiness of data**: To enable more confident decision making, research techniques and technologies to help assure the trustworthiness of data.

- **Cyberinfrastructure**: To drive innovation and support agency missions, build and enhance large-scale data cyberinfrastructure.

- **Data capture, curation, management, and access**: To increase the value of data; research and develop methods and technologies that provide scalable, automated, and sustainable ways to capture, curate, manage, and access it.

- **Data privacy, security, and ethics**: To provide security, protect privacy, and develop standard ethical practices regarding large-scale data collection, sharing, and use; research and develop appropriate safeguards, best practices, and standards.

- **Education and training**: To meet the demand for both deep analytical talent and analytical capacity for the broader workforce, research and develop large-scale data education and training.

- **Collaborations**: To build a resilient and effective large-scale data innovation ecosystem; create and enhance cross-agency, cross-sector, and cross-domain partnerships and collaborations.

Highlights of the Request

The LSDMA agencies report the following topical areas as highlights of their planned R&D investments for FY 2017. Agencies are listed in alphabetical order:

- **Next-generation capabilities and improved trustworthiness of data for decision making:** For all agencies dealing with large-scale and complex data, new ways are being sought to enable trustworthy and intuitive visualizations of data as well as effective analytical tools for decision makers. Highlights include:

- o **DARPA**: Big Mechanism, Deep Extraction from Text (DEFT), Probabilistic Programming for Advancing Machine Learning (PPAML), and Mining and Understanding Software Enclaves (MUSE) programs.

- o **DHS**: HSARPA Data Analytics Engine including the DHS on-site Multi-tenant Laboratory, support to S&T APEX programs, and DHS Component Analytics Activities.

- o **DOE/SC**: Advanced Scientific Computing Research (ASCR), Scientific Data Management, Analysis and Visualization for Extreme Scale Science (SDMAV) and as an integral part of DOE/SC's High Energy Physics (HEP) and Basic Energy Science (BES) programs.

- o **NARA**: Continued work in standards related to trustworthiness, including ISO 14721, ISO 16363, and ISO 16919.

- o **NIH**: Driving Data Science Innovation (new software tools for high need areas).

- o **NSF**: BIGDATA research program, Data for Scientific Discovery and Action (D4SDA) program, data science pilots, and individual directorate-led initiatives.

- **Cyberinfrastructure:** NSF's large-scale data cyberinfrastructure within the Data Infrastructure Building Blocks (DIBBs) component of the D4SDA program and DOE/SC's Advance Extreme Scale Science program. Both programs are relevant to improving coherence between the worlds of "big data and big compute." These programs must address the combined strengths and challenges of these often disparate computing environments to develop a capable exascale computing system that supports both simulation and data analysis at scale. – DOE/SC and NSF

- **Data capture, curation, management, and access:** NIH to support projects in digital resource discovery and indexing, data and metadata standards, making cloud/super-compute more accessible, and sustainability (storage of data). NIST to establish data best practices, reference frameworks, and reference datasets to enable new tools, drive foundational advances, and facilitate data sharing. – NARA, NIH, and NIST

- **Data privacy, security, and ethics:** DARPA's data privacy research program, Brandeis, seeks to develop the technical means to protect the private and proprietary information of individuals and enterprises. NIST works to develop standards, guidelines, best practices, and reference frameworks to enable reliability, security, and privacy protection. – DARPA and NIST

- **Education and training:** DHS, NSF, and NIH to nurture a data science community that provides education and training at multiple levels, including professional development within the existing workforce, and collaboration that reaches out to other research areas and grows the next generation. – DHS, NIH, and NSF

- **Collaboration:** Foster cross-agency and cross-sector collaboration - DHS to help grow a large-scale data innovation ecosystem through collaboration with industry, academia, and government programs and labs; NIH's BD2K Consortium; NIST's outreach to industry and Federal agencies in developing standards and best practices; NSF's BIGDATA programs and data science pilots. – DHS, NIH, NIST, and NSF

Planning and Coordination Supporting Request

Within a year of releasing the White House Big Data R&D Initiative in March 2012, OSTP directed the BD SSG to focus on collaborative efforts and partnerships that hold promise for leveraging large-scale data. The importance of collaboration is exemplified in the numerous ways that agencies reach out to other agencies and other entities for solutions. Highlights include:

- **DARPA**: Forty-eight separate collaboration partners including CIA, DoD, DOE, DOJ, DHS, HHS, NASA, NSA, ONR, USDA, and VA.

- **DHS**: Cross-department R&D such as with Immigration and Customs Enforcement (ICE), Transportation Security Administration (TSA), Federal Emergency Management Agency (FEMA), and others; monthly Big

Data (multiagency) workshops; with NSF on Big Data and the Center for Hybrid Multicore Processing Research; with NASA on low power processors; and with DARPA on XDATA; Cooperative Research And Development Agreements (CRADAs) for agreements with leading industry partners, and with In-Q-Tel Venture Capital.

- **DOE/SC**: Materials Genome Initiative (MGI); the U.S. Global Change Research Program (USGCRP), Big Data Initiative; DOE/NNSA on exascale and other agencies with NSCI; climate data sharing; Large Hadron Collider experimental and simulation data sharing and analysis (global collaborations); and analysis and feature detection in large volumes of synchrotron x-ray and neutron scattering data on structure and dynamics from complex materials (national collaboration).

- **NARA**: Working with OMB and others to ensure that Federal agencies meet requirements identified in the Managing Government Records Directive[12] focused on electronic recordkeeping. This includes a requirement to manage all email records in an electronic format by December 31, 2016.

- **NIH**: Coordination across agencies and countries on data access, sharing, and integration, challenges, prizes, and other collaborations; on questions of resource discovery, indexing, citation, and annotation across agencies and data types; and in the support of joint workshops and meetings in areas of common interest.

- **NIST**: Big Data Interoperability Framework; the ISO/IEC JTC 1/WG9 Working Group; the interagency Technical Advisory Group (iTAG); DARPA XDATA program; and the Center for Hierarchical Materials Design.

- **NSF**: BIGDATA program with the Office of Financial Research (OFR); workshops on Big Data and IoT with DHS; "Envisioning the Data Science Discipline" workshops (multiple partners); joint programs and workshops with NIH; Data Science Meetup groups.

The following topic areas are the priorities identified for collaboration for the upcoming fiscal year. These build on the shared vision and priorities of the participating agencies and the 2015 PCAST recommendations:

- Best practices and support structures for data capture, curation, management, and access

- Best practices for designing, initiating, managing, and maintaining big data projects

- Uses of machine learning to guide decision making

- Human understanding of large datasets and the results of their analysis

- Methods for representing and propagating error analyses and confidence measures

Planned coordination activities include NITRD sponsored multiagency workshop to bring together the Federal, private, and academic sectors to discuss best practices and support structures for data capture, curation, management, and access. The remaining topics will be explored using focused discussions and guest speakers at monthly meetings.

Additional 2016 and 2017 Activities by Agency

The following list provides a summary of individual agencies' ongoing programmatic interests for 2016 and 2017 under the LSDMA PCA.

- **DARPA**: Technologies are developed to enable processing of huge volumes of diverse, incomplete, uncertain, and often contradictory data in tactically relevant timeframes. Efforts address capability needs that include: conditioning of structured, semi-structured, and unstructured data; domain-specific search and

---

[12] OMB-NARA Memorandum - Managing Government Records Directive (M-12-18), August 24, 2012:
https://www.whitehouse.gov/sites/default/files/omb/memoranda/2012/m-12-18.pdf.
The Presidential Memorandum - Managing Government Records, issued on November 28, 2011, required the Directive.
https://www.whitehouse.gov/the-press-office/2011/11/28/presidential-memorandum-managing-government-records.

retrieval; content discovery, organization, and analysis; automated model-building, activity analysis, behavioral modeling, and pattern-of-life characterization; anomaly and manipulation detection; visualization; and privacy-preserving information sharing.

- **DHS**: Dynamic risk assessment, deep learning experiments, progressive analytics for mixed latency networks, blockchain-based data management and information sharing, heterogeneous cloud architectures, and experiment with high-capability computing resources developed under the NSCI.

- **DOE/SC**: Working Group on digital data, adoption of the Office of Science statement by other parts of DOE, ASCR Computer Science workshops and PI meetings; ASCR Next-Generation Networking workshops, High Energy Physics (HEP) partners with ASCR to address big data challenges.

- **NARA**: Continued work with ISO 14721, ISO 16363, ISO 16919, and related standards activities concerning trustworthy digital repositories; effective management of the Federal Government's digital assets; global-scale, open-source, next-generation technologies, architectures, and services enabling effective, sustainable management, intellectual control, and access to nationally distributed billion-file-and-larger-scale, complex digital object collections.

- **NIH**: Diversity (to strengthen diversity in the data science workforce), evaluation (to determine the impact of BD2K through new assessment tools), sustainability (to address the life cycle of data resources and how to assess and support them).

- **NIST**: Big data analytics ecosystem (to harmonize analytics architectures), big data discovery and reuse (extend the Commerce Interoperability Framework for data mashup), NIST data science evaluation (evaluation and benchmark methods for generalized data science and analytic problems), privacy engineering, and the MGI.

- **NSF**: D4SDA, Big Data Regional Innovation Hubs, Big Data Spokes solicitation, and Data Science Education workshops.

Large Scale Networking (LSN)

NITRD Agencies: DARPA, DoD (CERDEC, DREN), DoD Service Research Organizations (AFRL, AFOSR, ONR), DOE/SC, NASA, NIH, NIJ, NIST, NOAA, NSA, NSF, and OSD
Other Participants: FAA, FCC, USDA/ARS, and USGS

LSN focuses on R&D in leading-edge networking technologies, services, and enhanced performance. This includes programs in fundamental networking research and infrastructure, software defined networks, future Internet architectures, wireless networks, heterogeneous multimedia networks, testbeds, and end-to-end performance and performance measurement. Program coordination also spans network security, and identity management; dynamic inter-domain networking; public service networks; the science and engineering of complex networks; network infrastructures for advanced discovery environments; network-enabling technology; networking education, training, and outreach; and cyberinfrastructure for scientific and applications R&D.

LSN Coordination: For the LSN PCA, agencies coordinate their R&D activities through the Large Scale Networking Coordinating Group (LSN CG) and LSN teams: the Joint Engineering Team (JET) and Middleware And Grid Interagency Coordination (MAGIC) Team. Agencies may also coordinate through the High End Computing Interagency Working Group (HEC IWG) on crosscutting topics or activities related to large-scale networking infrastructure in support of high-capability computing (HCSIA PCA). For clarity, the association of a particular NITRD group with a particular coordination activity that crosscuts PCAs is provided below, as needed.

President's FY 2017 Request

Strategic Priorities Underlying This Request

The missions of the LSN agencies, though varied, all require ultra-high-speed communications, ultra-scale data-transfer capabilities, and virtualization and collaboration capabilities with demanding constraints on end-to-end performance, security, reliability, resilience, and availability. The advanced Federal research networks support national security and privacy needs, enable the transfer of data from scientific instruments, and transport data among the world's leading science centers and observational systems on the ground, on the seas, in the air, and in space. Each year, the LSN agencies identify a small number of priority areas in which focused research collaboration will promote advances in networking that address these needs and benefit all. The big data testbed, for example, identifies architectures and deploys best practices for transport of big data in support of advanced science applications. LSN collaborative activities for 2017 will focus on:

- **Enabling end-to-end big data applications**: Build on big data testbed demonstrations and expand the networking support of big data transfers, extend leading-edge network technology for big data, monitor network performance, and work with application users to improve end-to-end throughput, reliability, and security of big data transfers.

- **Operational capabilities**: Identify approaches, best practices, and testbed implementations for Software Defined Networking (SDN), Software Defined Infrastructure (SDI), and SDN Exchanges (SDXs), tactical communications and emerging network technologies (e.g., dynamic, ad hoc, multi-hop, secure, robust wireless networks and virtual/data-centric environments), low probability of detection and anti-jam networks, identity management, distributed computing, cloud computing, collaboration capabilities, spectrum management, IPv6, DNSSEC, science DMZ, Trusted Internet Connections (TICs), and perfSONAR.

- **Internet architecture**: Develop future Internet architecture, extreme data networking, cloud networking and services, multiple 100G networking and testbeds, and grid services supporting science research, collaborative science, and high performance computing.

Highlights of the Request

The LSN agencies report the following topical areas as highlights of their planned networking R&D investments for FY 2017. Agencies are listed in alphabetical order:

- **SDI, SDN, and SDN Internet Exchange Points (IXPs)**: Develop, deploy, and operate dynamic, secure, inter-domain, layers 1, 2, and 3 operational and virtualized networking capabilities. – AFRL, CERDEC, DOE/SC, NASA, NIST, NSA, NSF, and ONR

- **Network architectures and protocols for future networks (FIA-NP, GENI, NSFFutureCloud, NeTS, CIF21)**: Develop and test network architecture concepts to enable reliable, secure, flexible, and dynamic networking capabilities for heterogeneous, hybrid, and peer-to-peer networks; support sustainable environments, efficient Size, Weight, and Power (SWaP) networking, and virtualization at scale. – AFRL, CERDEC, DREN, DOE/SC, NASA, NIST, NSF, ONR, and OSD

- **Big data networking and infrastructure**: Provide end-to-end architectures integrated storage, applications, computational resources (e.g., science DMZ, SATCOM), and testbeds at differing scales (up to terabit-plus). Promote cooperation and test advanced applications on DOE/SC's 100/400 Gbps Advanced Networking Initiative (ANI), NSF's Global Environment for Networking Innovations (GENI), international 100+ Gbps testbeds, and other R&D testbeds to demonstrate performance at scale of new architectures (e.g., SDN) and end-to-end applications (e.g., US Ignite). – DOE/SC, DREN, NASA, NIST, NOAA, NSA, and NSF

- **Wireless networking**: Develop standards and tools enabling better interconnectivity, seamless multi-domain, heterogeneous, and layer interoperability; electronic warfare/communications coexistence and management for wideband (e.g., SWaP reduction, data fusion, heterogeneous interfaces, spectrum management and efficiency, sensing and sharing, low probability of detection, and anti-jam); robust, secure, resilient, dynamic, mobile, delay-tolerant networking (DTN), Shared Spectrum Access for Radar and Communication (SSPARC), RadioMap, spread-spectrum, Long Term Evolution (LTE) Advanced, WiFi, WiMAX, airborne, and sensor networks. – AFRL, CERDEC, DARPA, NASA, NIST, NSA, NSF, and ONR

- **Strategic technologies for networking**: Provide basic research, development, and demonstration of new and heterogeneous technologies for robust, secure, reliable, evolvable wired and wireless networking, underwater communications, autonomous dynamic ad hoc routing infrastructure, tactical and directional networking, medical devices, and assistive technologies. – CERDEC, DOE/SC, NIH, NIST, NSF, and ONR

- **Advanced discovery environments**: Provide grid and cloud services infrastructure that supports extreme-scale scientific knowledge discovery; provide security, management, and support for multi-domain collaborations, cyber-physical systems, data distribution and management, visualization, software stacks for large-scale scientific collaborations, high-bandwidth implementation, standards for smart grid interoperability, and testbeds; support for weather modeling, Open Science Grid (OSG), and Extreme Science and Engineering Discovery Environment (XSEDE). – DOE/SC, NASA, NIH, NIST, NOAA, NSA, and NSF

- **Computational research infrastructure (CC*DNI, IRNC, ESnet, N-Wave, science DMZ, Hawaii and Alaska connectivity, NIH medical database access)**: Provide networking to support U.S. and international research communities for networking research, large-scale data flows, end-to-end throughput, real-time networking, biomedical networking, and other applications. – DOE/SC, DREN, NASA, NIH, NIST, NOAA, and NSF

  Budget for computational research infrastructure is reported under the HCSIA PCA, but coordination is through the LSN CG. The LSN CG coordinates that portion of HCSIA that entails large-scale networking infrastructure in support of high-capability computing.

- **Energy aware and efficient networks**: Develop energy efficient technology and architectures for end-to-end big data applications, ad hoc mobile wireless and sensor networking, SWaP-efficient networking, and modeling for economic sustainability. – AFRL, CERDEC, DOE/SC, NSA, NSF, and ONR

- **End-to-end network management**: Enable cross-domain end-to-end performance measurement for advanced networking; enable autonomous secure management; provide tools for and implement performance measurement and services (e.g., perfSONAR). – CERDEC, DOE/SC, NASA, NIST, and NSF

- **Network security**: Develop technologies for detection of anomalous behavior; standards, modeling, and measurement to achieve end-to-end security over wireless networks and heterogeneous, multi-domain networks and infrastructure; critical infrastructure protection; DTN; trustworthy networking; protected SATCOM, cybersecurity defenses, IPv6, DNSSEC, TICs; authentication, policy, cryptography. – AFRL, CERDEC, DOE/SC, NASA, NIH, NIST, NSA, NSF, and ONR

- **Complexity in networking**: Develop concepts, methods, architectures, protocols, and measurement for modeling networks as complex, autonomous, and dynamic systems. – DOE/SC, NIST, and NSF

- **Public-safety networking, disaster recovery, and crisis management**: Provide Disaster Information Management Research Center (DIMRC), public-safety communications, implant communication system. – NIH (NLM) and NIST

Planning and Coordination Supporting Request

The LSN agencies have extensive experience working through interagency and private-sector partnerships to interconnect and extend the capabilities of federally supported research networks. For example, by engaging participants from academia, industry, national labs, and international networking groups, LSN's Joint Engineering Team is able to coordinate efforts at the global level to resolve technical networking issues and develop collaborative testbeds for exploring advanced technologies at scale. The following are ongoing LSN coordination activities:

- **Big data networking and demonstrations**: Networking and demonstrations for extreme-scale science and data flows; experimentation, network management, perfSONAR deployment; DTN; experimental design for complex systems; network performance measurement; network security; and GENI, OpenFlow, US Ignite, Smart and Connected Communities (S&CC), NIST Big Data Public Working Group (NBD-PWG), and SDN testing. – LSN agencies

- **Infrastructure cooperation**: National and trans-oceanic connectivity for scientific instrument access, data management, security, and performance measurement, TICs, TIC Access Providers (TICAPs). – DOE/SC, DREN, NASA, NOAA, and NSF

- **Application development**: GENI, US Ignite, S&CC, weather modeling, bioinformatics, standards. – DOE/SC, DREN, NIH, NIST, NOAA, and NSF

- **Multiagency workshops**: Science DMZ security best practices, SDN security progress, SDX implementations, deployments, and progress. – LSN agencies

- **400 Gbps/terabit networking research** – DOE/SC, NSF, and other LSN agencies

- **Inter-service collaboration (DoD)**: Research on robust, reliable, secure wireless and heterogeneous networking; spectrum access and management; SDN; DTN; dynamic spectrum access; The Technical Cooperation Program (TTCP); Joint Tactical Edge Networks Group; SATCOM; cybersecurity; services for federation, management, information, discovery, and secure delivery; modeling analysis and design; network performance; resilient tactical networks. – AFRL, CERDEC, and ONR

- **Software Defined Infrastructure**: Testing of SDN, SDX, IXP applications in at-scale testbeds. – DOE/SC, DREN, NASA, NIST, NSA, and NSF

- **End-to-end performance measurement, metrics** – DOE/SC, DREN, NASA, and NIST

- **Information exchange**: Multiagency participation in review panels, informational meetings, principal investigator (PI) meetings; coordination among program managers; and joint JET and Internet2 Joint Techs Meetings. – AFOSR, DOE/SC, NASA, NIST, NSA, NSF, and ONR

- **Coordination by LSN Teams**

  o **Joint Engineering Team (JET)**: Coordination of end-user requirements, science user interfaces, engineering of research networks and testbeds (JETnets); networking for advanced demonstrations; end-to-end big data transport and storage networks; security best practices, application testbeds (DNSSEC, IPv6, perfSONAR, and performance measurement), TIC/TICAP coordination; inter-domain and end-to-end metrics, monitoring; tool sharing and exchange; international coordination; and transit and services cooperation. – DOE/SC, DREN, NASA, NIH, NIST, NOAA, NSA, NSF, and ONR

  o **Middleware And Grid Interagency Coordination (MAGIC) Team**: Research for evolution of distributed computing, cloud and grid computing services, middleware; cloud and grid standards and implementation status (XSEDE, Open Science Grid); best practices for resource architecture, access, and management; security and privacy, e.g., identity management; and international coordination. – DOE/SC, NASA, NIST, and NSF

Additional 2016 and 2017 Activities by Agency

The following list provides a summary of individual agencies' ongoing programmatic interests for 2016 and 2017 under the LSN PCA:

- **AFRL**: Secure, multi-domain architectures, aerial layering networking, network and spectrum Command and Control (C2), reliable line of sight and beyond links, link survivability in contested environments, secure tactical intranet, multi-level security routing, directional data links and networking, robust communication infrastructure for nuclear C2.

- **CERDEC**: Mission continuity under cyberattacks, content-based networking, SATCOM on-the-move terminals, soldier radio waveform, real-time frequency management, protected SATCOM in contested environments, cellular-enabled communications, hardware convergence, next-generation Blue Force Tracking, tactical PKI, software-based encryption, directional networking, reprogrammable single-chip universal encryptor.

- **DARPA**: Develop and demonstrate system concepts and enabling technologies to provide assured high-bandwidth mobile wireless capabilities that match or exceed commercial wired infrastructure.

- **DOE/SC**: SDN/SDI research, extreme-scale scientific knowledge discovery, data generation to HPC connectivity, science applications over complex networks, cross-domain network monitoring and measurement, open exchange points (layers 1, 2, 3), big data demonstrations, trans-oceanic 100G network links, science DMZ.

- **DREN**: Network infrastructure (DREN III, SDN/SDI, IPv6, science DMZ, DNS, Network Transport Protocol, performance measurement), type 1 encryption, US Ignite over DREN, big data transfers, cybersecurity (science DMZ, Jigsaw security vulnerability assessment, risk management framework), Alaska and Hawaii connectivity, GENI nodes.

- **NASA**: SDN/SDX/Network Functions Virtualization (NFV), cloud services, IT security (intrusion protection, scalable perimeter protection, 100G monitoring, TIC, cyber defense), technologies (DTN, DMZ, IPv6, perfSONAR, big data distribution), Information Technology Infrastructure Integration Program (I3P).

- **NIH**: Advanced networking for health science research, 100G backbone network, network infrastructure for National Center for Biotechnology Information, Big Data to Knowledge (BD2K) networking, cloud technologies, career development and training, data commons.

- **NIST**: Next-generation network technologies (improved security and robustness), performance measurement, SDN, NFV, spectrum-efficient and public safety networking, science of complex information systems, cloud computing and big data standards and guidance, networked cyber-physical systems, data-driven discovery, Internet infrastructure protection, anti -DDOS technology, Communication Technology Laboratory (metrology, materials capabilities).

- **NOAA**: 100G N-Wave new technology, X-wave (TICAP, 100G), Dispersion compensation dense wavelength division multiplexing (DC DWDM) ring, NOAA DMZ, network infrastructure for next-generation weather modeling supercomputing, instrument support (Joint Polar Satellite System [JPSS], Geostationary Operational Environmental Satellite R-Series [GOES-R] program), international data partnership connectivity, multicast data transport with the European Organisation for the Exploitation of Meteorological Satellites (EUMETSAT).

- **NSA**: SDN/IXP/NFV, SDN security, SDN prototype, cloud networking (Accumulo, OpenStack open source community), cyber defense at scale, extreme data networking (Tbps, low SWaP, fusion analytics), IoT capability.

- **NSF**: Basic network science and research, wireless (technology, spectral efficiency), NeTS (enterprise, core, optical, wireless, mobile, cellular networks); resilient smart grids, clouds, data centers; optical and photonic systems; Future Internet Architecture (FIA)- Next Phase: prototype demonstrations, encompass societal/economic/legal issues, security; GENI (LTE, WiFi, transition to communities), NSFFutureCloud (architecture infrastructure, cloud-based applications, CloudLab and Chameleon infrastructure and storage, extension to GENI infrastructure, community/industry interaction); US Ignite and S&CC; XSEDE advanced infrastructure, OSG high throughput computational services; international research connectivity (Asia, Americas, Europe, Africa); CIF21 integrated scalable infrastructure, Resource Public Key Infrastructure (RPKI) routing security; international SDN/WAN testbeds, workshops on transition of technology.

- **ONR**: Spectrum- and energy-efficient radios and apertures, tactical communications (high bandwidth optical and wireless, dynamic spectrum access, underwater links for sensors); tactical networks (dynamic ad hoc, multi-hop, wireless technology that is robust to link disruptions, long battery life networked sensors), SDN, Applied Research Challenge (spread spectrum), Virtualized Network Operations Center(Speed-to-Fleet initiative); Dynamic Tactical Communications Network (DTCN)/Automated Digital Network System (ADNS) interoperability demonstration.

Robotics and Intelligent Systems (RIS)

NITRD Agencies: DoD Service Research Organizations, NASA, NIH, NIJ, NIST, NSF, and OSD
Other Participants: DOE/EM and USDA/NIFA

RIS R&D focuses on advancing physical and computational agents that complement, expand, or emulate human physical capabilities or intelligence. This includes robotics hardware and software design, application, and practical use; machine perception; intelligent cognition, adaptation, and learning; mobility and manipulation; human-robot interaction; distributed and networked robotics; increasingly autonomous systems; and related applications. RIS provides visibility into robotics R&D and supporting technologies drawn from artificial intelligence.

Research and commercial opportunities in systems that couple IT technologies with sensing and actuation—from the IoT to smart infrastructure to robotics—are evolving rapidly. Researchers in robotics, artificial intelligence, cyber-physical systems, and related areas will drive innovation in basic IT, as well as the development of robust, reliable autonomous systems that incorporate advanced sensing and sensors. As new products and technologies emerge for IT-enabled sensing and acting in the physical world, it becomes important to establish open standards and platforms to encourage the sharing of new technologies with and among the research community. Research is needed to focus on human interaction with systems that operate in the physical world, particularly around issues of safety, trust, and predictability of response. Additional research is needed in areas such as physical IT and human interaction, physical IT and robust autonomy, physical IT and sensing, the development of hardware and software abstractions for physical IT systems, and trustworthy physical IT systems.

RIS Coordination: For the RIS PCA, agencies will coordinate their R&D activities through a new NITRD group that is being established (to be named). Agencies may also coordinate through the High Confidence Software and Systems Coordinating Group (HCSS CG) or Human Computer Interaction and Information Management Coordinating Group (HCI&IM CG) on crosscutting topics or activities in robotics and intelligent systems. For clarity, the association of a particular NITRD group with a particular coordination activity that crosscuts PCAs is provided below, as needed.

President's FY 2017 Request

Because the RIS PCA is a new PCA for FY 2017 and no existing NITRD group previously supported agency coordination across the full RIS scope, RIS reporting for the FY 2017 request is focused on the National Robotics Initiative (NRI). A new NITRD group is being established to support future interagency coordination of RIS R&D activities. For those NITRD agencies reporting and providing information on RIS programs outside the NRI, information is provided below by agency.

Planning and Coordination Supporting Request

Coordination under RIS for FY 2017 is ongoing in the following area:

- **National Robotics Initiative (NRI)**: Cross-cutting program to accelerate the development and use of robots that work beside, or cooperatively with, people. Innovative robotics research and applications emphasizing the realization of such co-robots working in symbiotic relationships with human partners is supported by multiple agencies. – DoD, DOE/EM, NASA, NIH, NSF, and USDA/NIFA

  Budget for the NRI is reported under the RIS PCA, but the HCSS CG previously coordinated that portion of RIS that entails the safe, dependable operation of robots developed and used cooperatively with people. The HCI&IM CG previously coordinated that portion of RIS that emphasizes the realization of co-robots acting in direct support of, or in a symbiotic relationship with, human partners.

Additional 2016 and 2017 Activities by Agency

The following list provides a summary of individual agencies' ongoing programmatic interests for 2016 and 2017 under the RIS PCA:

- **AFRL:** Research and technologies to enable effective teams of distributed operators and increasingly intelligent autonomous systems; to include flexible task delegation and control for human-autonomy interaction, automation transparency/feedback displays, adaptive autonomy, intuitive user interface methods, and methods for influencing trust; resulting in highly effective human-autonomy teams with shared awareness, calibrated trust, and fewer personnel operating multiple autonomous systems.

- **DOE/EM:** Robotics research and technology development for: 1) handling of high-hazard, high-consequence materials and waste, 2) performing worker/operator tasks that are dirty (contaminated, toxic, nuisance), dull (routine, labor-intensive, repetitive, mundane), and dangerous (pose significant occupational hazards); 3) easing the performance of worker/operator tasks that are physically demanding on or stressful to human body or are otherwise ergonomically challenging; 4) performing tasks that are beyond human abilities; 5) improving the ability to response to and recover from unplanned events or operational emergencies; and 6) improving the safety, quality, efficiency, and productivity of facility operations. R&D areas of interest for the application of DOE/EM robotics technologies include, but are not limited to, remote access; non-destructive testing and evaluation; imaging, surveying, mapping, and 3-D rendering; manipulation and end-effectors; worker assistance; heavy operations; and task automation.

- **NASA**: Technologies to assist NASA's missions on and above Earth, in space, and on other worlds, including interaction between humans, robots, and autonomous systems. For human exploration, technologies include precursor systems, crew assistants, and caretakers. For aeronautics, technologies include unmanned aerial systems, cockpit assistants, and intelligent airspace management. For science missions, technologies include systems for sample acquisition, measurement, and in-situ analysis. Core technologies include sensing and perception, mobility, manipulation, human-system interaction, system-level autonomy, autonomous rendezvous and docking, and robotic systems engineering.

- **NIH**: Research and development of technologies to accelerate the next generation of adaptable robotics including: robotics for homecare and long-term personalized care that promote health and wellness; robotics for behavioral therapies and assistance in mobility, manipulation, visual improvements, human communication and cognition; and robotics that help eliminate health disparities across populations.

- **NIST**: Measurement science research to drive innovation and reduce risks of adoption of robotic technologies to improve manufacturing performance and emergency response effectiveness and safety. Research areas include: performance measurement of perception, mobility, dexterity, and safety technologies and systems; performance of collaborative robotic systems; agility performance of robotic systems; robotic systems interoperability and integration; metrics and tools to ease adoption of robotic technologies by small- and medium-sized manufacturers; and emergency response robot performance metrics, test methods, and standards. Robots and innovative robotic technologies are also developed and used in NIST measurement science research, such as robots built specifically to emulate human behavior by presenting artificial fingerprints to digital fingerprint scanners (for testing scanner repeatability), and high-precision and configurable scanning for measuring antenna performance at millimeter wavelengths.

- **ONR**: Machine Learning, Reasoning, and Intelligence program to develop principles of machine intelligence, efficient computational methods, algorithms, and tools for building versatile smart agents that can perform missions autonomously with minimal human supervision and collaborate seamlessly with teams of warfighters and other agents. The program is concerned with building intelligent agents that can function in the environments in which warfighters operate (i.e., unstructured, open, complex, and dynamically changing). A focus of ONR's cybersecurity research is to build the fundamental science and technologies needed to achieve Autonomic Cyber Systems (ACS), including computing machinery and communication and networking infrastructure. An ACS is an automated system that closes the loop of sensing, analyzing, planning, and taking action at cyber speed (computer as robot). An ACS employs machine-situational awareness and advanced machine reasoning to understand its operating status and environment, plan for actions, and mitigate and inoculate against cyber exploits.

- **OSD**: R&D effort to develop machine perception that is relatable to the way a human perceives an environment; to integrate machine semantic understanding, reasoning, and perception into a ground robotic system; to develop intelligent ISR capability for sensing platforms; to develop a flexible UAV operator interface; to develop goal-directed reasoning, machine learning, and operator interaction techniques to enable management of UAV teams; to develop integrated human sensing capabilities to enable the human-machine team; and to develop small UAV teaming algorithms to enable systems to autonomously search a cave.

Social, Economic, and Workforce Implications of IT and IT Workforce Development (SEW)

NITRD Agencies: DHS, DoD Service Research Organizations (AFRL, ARL, NRL, ONR), DOE/NNSA, DOE/SC, NASA, NIH, NIST, NSF, and OSD
Other Participants: BLS, ED, IARPA, and USDA

Research activities funded under the SEW PCA focus on the co-evolution of IT and social, economic, and workforce systems, including interactions between people and IT and among people developing and using IT in groups, organizations, and larger social networks. Collaborative science concerns are addressed including understanding and improving the effectiveness of teams and enhancing geographically distributed, interdisciplinary R&D to engage societal concerns, such as competitiveness, security, economic development, and wellbeing. Workforce concerns are addressed by leveraging interagency efforts to improve education outcomes through the use of learning technologies that anticipate the educational needs of individuals and society. SEW also supports efforts to speed the transfer of R&D results to the policymaker, practitioner, and IT user communities in all sectors.

> **SEW Coordination**: For the SEW PCA, agencies coordinate their R&D activities through the Social, Economic, and Workforce Implications of IT and IT Workforce Development Coordinating Group (SEW CG) and SEW teams: SEW-Collaboration, SEW-Education, and Social Computing.

President's FY 2017 Request

Strategic Priorities Underlying This Request

Priorities in SEW reflect the sweeping socio-technical transformations occurring as a result of 21st century life in an increasingly networked society. From crowdsourcing to e-science to cyberlearning, new forms of social collaboration and non-traditional problem-solving methods increasingly leverage networked, online environments. In cyberspace, thousands voluntarily contribute time and intellectual resources for collective tasks, such as writing open-source software, citizen science, and identifying words in non-machine-readable text. Global cross-disciplinary teams connected through cyberinfrastructure play a central role in addressing societal needs, such as developing economical solar power, mitigating environmental disasters, delivering new medical interventions, and maintaining our national security. A new era of human-machine partnerships is emerging, and much research is needed to understand how to harness these novel forms of collective action most effectively and efficiently. In this new era, developing cyber-capable citizens is also critical – from the ability to use digital capabilities wisely and effectively to the IT skills and knowledge needed in the advanced technical workforce of tomorrow. It is imperative that the general population be able to understand the challenges in complex systems, such as in healthcare information infrastructures, e-commerce, and computing, and to balance trade-offs with respect to privacy, security, and reliability. Emerging concerns in cyber-social behavior also need to be addressed. The rise of militant actors, information conflicts, and significant phenomena in crowd hysteria and social manipulation require research and technology to support human welfare and security. Developing cyber-social sciences is a key to achieving balance between societal needs and concerns. SEW priorities exemplify the scope of these concerns among the NITRD agencies. Many SEW activities involve extending understanding and applications of IT to help people learn, conduct research, and innovate more effectively. Key focus areas include:

- **Collaboration**
  - **Increase fundamental knowledge**: Advance understanding of how to efficiently and effectively manage, conduct, fund, and reward science teams collaborating with and through cyberinfrastructure by

developing evidence-based approaches to influence decision making and providing guiding principles and possible strategies in investing in effective and impactful collaborative research.

- o **Integrated multidisciplinary research**: Support empirical research, development, and education to improve capabilities for solving societal challenges using a systems-based approach to generate new solutions to complex problems and to understand, predict, and react to changes in the interconnected natural, social, and built environment. Multidisciplinary science teams especially hold promise for making progress and scientific breakthroughs in climate change, energy, health, education, security, and technology.

- **Education**

  - o **Transform science teaching and learning across educational settings**: Integrate computing in Science, Technology, Engineering, and Mathematics (STEM) education and use IT innovations to improve learning in the disciplines. Bring new data and evidence-based practices, content, knowledge, and real-world applications to more learners in all educational settings. Provide evidence-based professional development and support to STEM educators in the classroom to improve STEM instruction and retain effective teachers.

  - o **Preparing effective STEM teachers**: Recruit, prepare, retrain, and support talented individuals with strong content knowledge to become effective STEM teachers; engage STEM teachers in influencing the design and development of educational technologies (EdTech) and in understanding evidence on learning styles to use to teach effectively in IT-enabled learning settings that go beyond the classroom.

  - o **Research learning and cognition**: Promote the integration of research and understanding of how the brain learns. Address challenges of translating scientific understanding to the classroom. Understand the role of time and timing in learning, brain systems, and social systems to develop a new science of the temporal dynamics of learning. Understand the fundamental processes that underlie human learning by studying dynamic interactions within and among brain regions. Promote pedagogies that improve skills and competencies at all education levels that integrate systems and computational thinking.

  - o **Workforce readiness**: Develop innovative approaches to broaden interest and participation in 21st century IT and computing careers, including information assurance, computer security, predictive science, and multicore computing technologies. Foster partnerships with academia and industry.

- **Social computing**

  - o **Increase fundamental knowledge**: Cyber-social behavior impacts human activity, drives events, and provides opportunities and challenges for U.S. Government missions in many critical areas. Research is needed to understand shifts in social dynamics that follow from cyber-social behavior, including disaster assessment, response and recovery, health and welfare assessments, humanitarian aid, cyber-diplomacy, the impact of online media and social platforms on human security, law enforcement, and the impact of the deep web. Research is also needed to advance understanding of the implications of Internet-based learning; the future of education, training, and learning in cyber-environments; social cognition and cognitive vulnerability in cyberspace; and the impact of new economic and social modalities such as block chain technologies, GPS-enabled migration, and other novel cyber-social and cyber-economic technical advances.

  - o **Cross-agency coordination and engagement**: Develop opportunities for cross-agency engagement and information sharing to coordinate research needs and requirements. Share understanding of ongoing and planned efforts in social computing research and find critical technical gaps. Critical mission spaces to be addressed include: defense, law enforcement, social service, humanitarian assistance, disaster response and recovery, diplomacy, international aid, and health.

- o **Transform scientific research collaborations across disparate disciplines**: Promote integrated, trans-disciplinary research that reaches across the "hard" and "soft" sciences to address the critical technical gaps, key questions, and problems of detecting, analyzing, and developing a holistic understanding of cyber-social behavior. Develop meetings and create challenge problems in forecast modeling, event detection, and analysis to better understand multi-scale narratives, information flow, and media impact and cyber-social dynamics.

Highlights of the Request

The SEW agencies report the following topical areas as highlights of their planned R&D investments for FY 2017. Agencies are listed in alphabetical order:

- **Collaboration**

  - o **Cross-disciplinary centers, institutes, communities and platform**: Support collaborative activities to advance a field or create new directions in research or education by providing a platform to enable coordination of research, training, and educational activities across disciplinary, organizational, geographic, and international boundaries. Create centers to coordinate multiyear activities addressing national challenges such as big data, translational sciences, energy efficiency, environmental sustainability, advanced communication, transportation, learning, and healthcare systems. – DOE/NNSA, NASA, NIH, and NSF

  - o **Cyber-human systems**: Focus on the co-evolution of social and technical systems to create new knowledge about human-machine partnerships and of the purposeful design of such systems, including e-science collaboration tools, human-robot partnerships, cyber-physical systems, advanced manufacturing, cyber-enabled materials, manufacturing and smart systems, and handling big data. – NASA, NIH, and NSF

  - o **Collaboration data**: Explore agency and research datasets on scientific collaboration studies and expand access to all datasets including sociometric badges, social media, and trace data. Leverage, analyze, share, and crosslink datasets to measure outcomes. – NASA, NIH, and NSF

- **Education**

  - o **Learning with educational technologies**: Understand advanced learning technologies that have demonstrated potential to transform STEM teaching and learning at all levels across all societal settings; understand technologies that can contribute to a highly interdisciplinary technical STEM workforce; enable new avenues of STEM learning with novel, collaborative, and global learning experiences for students, the general public, and the emerging IT workforce; advance the Nation's ability to study the learning process discretely and rapidly deploy new understandings and adaptive and assistive resources in education to broaden participation of all Americans in STEM R&D, including returning disabled veterans. – ED and NSF

  - o **Computing in STEM education**: Enable the study of pedagogies that will effectively integrate computing in STEM education to address the critical need for a future workforce literate and competent in computational and real-world problem-solving in support of the Nation's global competitiveness. – NSF

  - o **Cybersecurity education**: Bolster formal education programs to focus on cybersecurity and STEM. – ED, NIST, and NSF

  - o **Cybersecurity workforce training and professional development**: Intensify training and professional development programs for the existing cybersecurity workforce. – NIST, NSF, and other agencies

- **Social computing**

  - **Cross-agency research and development engagement**. Share agency investments in existing Social Computing programs and initiatives across Federal agencies. Make available knowledge and tools to foster sharing of agency strategies and the funding of cross-agency R&D efforts. – DHS, DoD, NASA, NSF, ONR, OFR, USAID, and DHS/USSS

  - **Facilitate multidisciplinary research**. Provide opportunities for social computing and cyber-social researchers to expand their awareness of trans-disciplinary methods, data, and resources and to work together on developing novel approaches combining hard and soft sciences.

Planning and Coordination Supporting Request

The SEW Coordinating Group (SEW CG) continues to pursue opportunities for expanded interagency collaborations to improve IT education and workforce training, team science, and social computing.

Collaboration: The SEW-Collab Team plans to engage agencies in developing best practices for planning, awarding, and evaluating large collaborative proposals.

Education: The SEW-Ed Team continues to track the reorganization of Federal STEM education programs, as outlined in the Federal STEM Education 5-Year Strategic Plan.[13] The Plan identifies NSF, ED, and the Smithsonian Institution as the lead agencies for Federal STEM education programs, and calls for engaging government, academia, and industry to introduce curricula that can satisfy specific industry and government workforce needs.

Social computing: The Social Computing Team plans to focus on and coordinate efforts that emphasize cognitive security, prediction markets, sentiment analysis, crisis informatics, and human security. A workshop on social computing and human security is being planned for fall 2016.

Additional 2016 and 2017 Activities by Agency

The following list provides a summary of individual agencies' ongoing programmatic interests for 2016 and 2017 under the SEW PCA:

- **DHS**: Provide institutions with an information assurance or computer security curriculum in a controlled, competitive environment to assess students' depth of understanding and operational competency in managing the challenges inherent in protecting corporate network infrastructures and business information systems. Reduce the shortage in today's cyber workforce by serving as the premier program that identifies, attracts, recruits, and places the next generation of cybersecurity professionals. The U.S. Cyber Challenge (USCC) fosters partnerships and sponsorships that support students and professionals who want to help protect vital U.S. cyber assets and infrastructure.

- **DOE/NNSA**: Critical-skills development of university participants in the Advanced Simulation and Computing (ASC) Alliance Program and training of next-generation computational scientists in the DOE Computational Science Graduate Fellowship program. Train future scientists to work on the kinds of interdisciplinary teams that are demanded by today's challenges.

- **DOE/SC**: Maintain a healthy pipeline of computational scientists equipped and trained to address DOE's mission needs, including advances in exascale computing, by supporting the Computational Science Graduate Fellowship program.

- **NIH**: Promote the use of technologies that improve educational outcomes of both trainees and established scientists by facilitating the efficient acquisition of knowledge and skills. Increase knowledge of scientific

---

[13] *Federal Science, Technology, Engineering, and Mathematics (STEM) Education 5-Year Strategic Plan*, May 2013, NSTC: http://www.whitehouse.gov/sites/default/files/microsites/ostp/stem_stratplan_2013.pdf.

workforce dynamics in areas critical to advancing the NIH mission by developing evidence-informed policy decisions. Provide grants to support programs that provide integrated training in computer science, the quantitative sciences, and biomedicine. Awards support an effective and diverse biomedical data science workforce by supporting educational resource development, training opportunities, and public engagement projects.

- **NIST**: Develop a framework to provide a common understanding of, and lexicon for, cybersecurity work. The use of standardized terms to consistently define cybersecurity work is essential to our ability to educate, recruit, train, develop, and retain a highly qualified workforce.

- **NSF**: Advance new modes of collective intelligence (e.g., social, participatory, and intelligent computing) while also ensuring that human values are embedded in these emerging systems and infrastructures; support the human capital essential for advances across all disciplines by linking key areas of educational investments in high-capability computing systems, data, education, software, virtual organizations, networking, and campus bridging; broaden participation in computing by underrepresented minorities; support faculty, graduate, and undergraduate fellowships, traineeships, and junior faculty; promote digital gaming in education; Discovery Research K-12 (DRK-12) program for significant and sustainable improvements in STEM learning, advance STEM teaching, and contribute to improvements in the Nation's formal education system.

- **ONR**: With OSD, develop improved understanding of human and social aspects of cyberspace, including information conflicts, cyber-diplomacy and community engagement in cyberspace, disaster and humanitarian assistance, and the new information environment. Advance and develop improvements in training for future cyber defense and civil affairs in social computing related to human security issues. International collaboration: ONR and ARL participate in international research collaborations associated with NATO Allied Transformation Command activities relevant to social computing. ONR activities include research collaborations with the Defence Science and Technology Group (Australia), Defence Science and Technology Laboratory (United Kingdom), and the Netherlands Organisation (TNO) for Applied Scientific Research (Human Factors 241, Information Technology, Disaster Management and Crisis). ARL and AFRL participate in the NATO Information Systems Technology Panel on Content-Based Analytics with TNO and Canada's Defense Research and Development agency.

Software Design and Productivity (SDP)

NITRD Agencies: DHS, DoD Service Research Organizations (AFRL, ONR), DOE/SC, NASA, NIH, NIST, NOAA, NSA, NSF, and OSD
Other Participants: BLS, FDA, and NRC

A computational revolution is transforming industry and society, driven by software operating and interacting with physical, personal, and social environments. Software and the possibilities for computational behaviors are transforming every facet of every industry. Products that are not computational are dependent upon computationally intensive simulation-based engineering and science (SBE&S) or manufactured by computational machinery. Pervasive computational behaviors present enormous opportunities for industry and society, but also pose significant challenges. Current technology works quite well in many familiar domains of modest scale, as long as the error-prone characteristic of current software is accepted. The cost of these errors includes increased vulnerability of the software to cyber-attack and waste that is significant on a national scale. Meeting these challenges requires solving the intellectually deep, difficult, and important problems in the science, mathematics, and engineering of computational behaviors, information processes, and software representations.

The SDP R&D agenda spans the science and the technology of software creation and sustainment (e.g., development methods and environments, V&V technologies, component technologies, languages, and tools) and software project management in diverse domains. R&D will advance software engineering concepts, methods, techniques, and tools that result in more usable, dependable, cost-effective, evolvable, and sustainable software-intensive systems. The domains cut across information technology, industrial production, evolving areas such as the Internet, and highly complex, interconnected software-intensive systems. The core SDP R&D activities are software productivity, software quality, software cost, responsiveness to change, and sustainment. The success of these activities can have a major beneficial effect on high-confidence systems because such systems are critically dependent upon the quality of the software and on the many companies producing software-reliant products. Moreover, software drives today's economy. The ability to quickly and affordably create and sustain quality software is critical to advancing U.S. productivity and innovation.

> **SDP Coordination**: For the SDP PCA, agencies coordinate their R&D activities through the Software Design and Productivity Coordinating Group (SDP CG).

President's FY 2017 Request

Strategic Priorities Underlying This Request

Complex software-based systems today power the Nation's most advanced defense, security, and economic capabilities. Such systems also play central roles in science and engineering discovery and, thus, are essential in addressing this century's grand challenges (e.g., low-cost, carbon-neutral, and renewable energy; clean water; next-generation health care; extreme manufacturing; space exploration, etc.). These large-scale systems typically must remain operational, useful, and relevant for decades. The involved agencies are working to identify and define the core elements for a new science of software development that will make engineering decisions and modifications transparent and traceable throughout the software lifecycle (e.g., design, development, evolution, and sustainment). A key goal of this science framework is to enable software engineers to maintain and evolve complex systems cost-effectively and correctly long after the original developers have departed. This new science of software development will also benefit the many companies producing software-reliant products that comprise an increasing portion of the economy. The following areas are research priorities:

- **Secure and Productive Software Development Grand Challenge:** Provide the technical capabilities to thwart and reverse adversaries' asymmetrical advantages with sustainably secure software development. The Secure and Productive Software Development Grand Challenge focuses on developing fast, affordable, low defect software production and sustainment technology usable by current software developers and inserting it into important application domains [e.g., Health apps, Smart and Connected Communities [S&CC], Software-defined infrastructure [SDI]).

- **Improve High Performance Computing (HPC) application developer productivity**: New approaches to building, sustaining, assuring, and programming HPC systems that make it possible to express programs at more abstract levels and then automatically map them onto specific machines. Foster the transition of improved development tools into actual practice, making the development, sustainment, and assurance of applications for HPC systems no more difficult than it is for other classes of large-scale systems.

- **Research to rethink software design**: From the basic concepts of design, evolution, and adaptation to advanced systems that seamlessly integrate human and computational capabilities, including:

  - **Foundational/core research on science and engineering of software:** Develop new computational models and logics, techniques, languages, tools, metrics, and processes for developing and analyzing software for complex software-intensive systems (e.g., a fundamental approach to software engineering that can provide systems that are verifiably correct, assured, efficient, effective, reliable, and sustainable).

  - **Next-generation software concepts, methods, and tools:** Reformulation of the development process, the tool chain, the partitioning of tasks and resources; open technology development (open-source and open-systems methods); technology from nontraditional sources; multidisciplinary and crosscutting concepts and approaches; and next-generation software concepts, methods, and tools will be needed for emerging technologies such as multicore, software-as-a-service, cloud computing, end-user programming, quantum information processing; and modeling of human-machine systems.

  - **Capabilities for building evolvable, sustainable, long-lived software-intensive systems:** Exploration of new means to create, keep current, and use engineering artifacts to support long-lived software-intensive systems; new approaches to reliably meet changing requirements and assure security and safety; and long-term retention and archiving of software-development data and institutional knowledge.

- **Explore fundamental principles:** Understand, design, analyze, and build software systems that are verifiable, regardless of size, scale, complexity, and heterogeneity, and are correct, assured, efficient, effective, and predictable. Build foundations of software for emerging quantum information science and quantum information processing.

- **Develop predictable, timely, cost-effective software-intensive systems**: Disciplined methods, technologies, and tools for systems and software engineering, rapidly evaluating alternative solutions to address evolving needs; measuring, predicting, and controlling software properties and tradeoffs; virtualized and model-based development environments; automation of deterministic engineering tasks; and scalable analysis, test generation, optimization, and verification with traceability to requirements; related issues include:

  - **Software application interoperability and usability**: Develop interface and integration standards, representation methods to enable software interoperability, data exchanges, interoperable databases; supply-chain system integration; and standardized software engineering practices for model development.

  - **Cost and productivity issues in development of safety-critical, embedded, and autonomous systems:** Research on composition, reuse, power tools, training, and education to address systems that can be inaccessible after deployment (e.g., spacecraft) and need to operate autonomously.

- **Transform SDP frontiers:** Invest in challenging, potentially transformative research; prepare and engage a diverse STEM workforce; sharpen the merit-review process to better identify such research; emphasize interdisciplinary and system-oriented approaches that can lead to transformational concepts.

- **Improve health IT interoperability:** Improve conformance testing, testability, and community knowledge of specifications.

- **Advance supply chain interoperability for digital manufacturing research**: Use model-based engineering, product manufacturing information standards, and systems engineering standards.

- **Assess software quality**: Provide reference datasets and test programs for software assurance and metrics.

- **Focus on Smart Grid security guidelines**: Support the multidisciplinary aspects of Smart Grid security.

Highlights of the Request

The SDP agencies report the following topical areas as highlights of their planned R&D investments for FY 2017. Agencies are listed in alphabetical order:

- **Software Infrastructure for Sustained Innovation (SI^2)**: Agency-wide program for development and integration of next-generation software infrastructure to advance scientific discovery and education at all levels in the sciences, mathematics, and engineering. – NSF

- **Cyberinfrastructure Framework for 21st Century Science and Engineering (CIF21)**: Development of new algorithms, tools, and other applications to support innovation. – NSF

- **Software and hardware foundations**: Scientific and engineering principles and new logics, languages, architectures, and tools for specifying, designing, programming, analyzing, and verifying software and software-intensive systems; formal methods; V&V tools for sound development of reliable and assured software; formal definitions of weaknesses; standards for certification; and techniques that enable prediction of cost and schedule for large-scale software projects. – AFRL, NASA, NIST, NOAA, NSF, ONR, and OSD

- **Computer systems research**: Rethink and transform the software stack for computer systems in different application domains (e.g., new reference architectures for embedded systems); investigate systems that involve computational, human/social, and physical elements. – AFRL, NASA, NIST, NSF, ONR, and OSD

- **Intelligent software design**: Investigate approaches to design software-intensive systems that operate in complex, real-time, distributed, and unpredictable environments; invariant refinement of software properties; automation and scaling of testing, validation, and system-level verification; automated analysis of model-based software development; transformational approaches to drastically reduce software life-cycle costs, complexity, and to extend life span; languages and modeling tools that support interoperability, data exchange among engineering tools, large-scale simulations, and federated information systems. – AFRL, NASA, NIST, NOAA, NSF, ONR, and OSD

- **Interoperability standards, knowledge capture processes**: Develop representation schemes for interoperability among computer-aided engineering systems; standards for instrument, mathematical, and measurement data; ontological approaches to facilitate integrating supply-chain systems; interoperability of databases; interoperability testing tools – NIST; and infrastructure for capture, reuse of domain expertise. – NOAA, ONR, and OSD

- **Cyber-Enabled Materials, Manufacturing, and Smart Systems (CEMMSS)**: NSF is to develop several comprehensive, integrated programs across the focus areas, e.g., in cyber-manufacturing, advanced materials, and smart systems, to encourage new connections, discoveries, and/or emerging fields of science and engineering. Progress towards CEMMSS goals will show evidence of: 1) an integrated and thriving ecosystem of cyber-enabled systems and advanced materials; 2) improved interdisciplinary education based on longitudinal study of education outcomes; and 3) advanced research infrastructure used by CEMMSS scientists and engineers. NSF expects to continue to grow the cyber-manufacturing program, building upon NSF core programs through the development and use of robust, reliable, usable, and sustainable software. – DoD, DOE, DOT, NIST, and NSF

- **Quantum Information Sciences**: Support Federal S&T Quantum Information Sciences IWG. – NIST

Planning and Coordination Supporting Request

The SDP agencies' current collaboration activities focus on domain areas in which large-scale, software-intensive, and cyber-physical systems predominate – such as in aviation, air-traffic control, and global climate and weather modeling – and on building a forward-looking research agenda to improve the engineering and evolution of such systems. NITRD agencies sponsor workshops to ensure collaboration among the government, industry, and academia (e.g., NSF CPS PI, NSF Secure and Trustworthy Cyberspace [SaTC] PI, and Computational Science and Engineering Software Sustainability and Productivity [CSESSP] Challenges workshops).

- **Software verification and validation**: Ongoing collaboration to develop effective approaches for next-generation air transportation. – AFRL, NASA, ONR, and OSD

- **Articulate SDP national needs, opportunities, and priorities:** Provide a focus for the future of software engineering research, and discuss and formulate software and productivity research goals and priorities. – SDP agencies

- **Earth System Modeling Framework (ESMF), weather research, and forecasting**: Long-term multiagency efforts to build, use common software toolset, data standards; visualization for weather and climate applications. – DoD Service research organizations, DOE/SC, NASA, NOAA, and NSF

- **Automatic program and processor synthesis for data-dependent applications:** From high-level mathematical description, generate code with performance comparable to hand-written code. – ONR

- **Automated combinatorial testing of software systems**: Methodology and infrastructure for automated testing that reduces the number of tests. – NASA and NIST

- **Next-generation aircraft**: Collaboration on concepts, modeling, and simulation tools. – DoD Service research organizations, NASA, and OSD

Additional 2016 and 2017 Activities by Agency

The following list provides a summary of individual agencies' ongoing programmatic interests for 2016 and 2017 under the SDP PCA:

- **AFRL:** Research is driven by the strategic goals of the "Autonomy Community of Interest (COI), Test and Evaluation, Verification and Validation (TEVV) Investment Strategy 2015-2018," released June 2015.[14] Goals include: 1) Methods and Tools Assisting in Requirements Development and Analysis, 2) Evidence-Based Design and Implementation, 3) Cumulative Evidence through Research, Developmental, and Operational Testing, 4) Run Time Behavior Prediction and Recovery, and 5) Assurance Arguments for Autonomous Systems. As a result of the strategy, the Test Resource Management Center (TRMC) - Unmanned Autonomous Systems Test (UAST) group is investigating how to change the Test and Evaluation (T&E) infrastructure to accommodate future autonomous systems. Additionally, AFRL in partnership with the OSD Scientific Test and Analysis Techniques in Test & Evaluation Center of Excellence (STAT in T&E COE)

---

[14] "DoD Autonomy COI Test and Evaluation, Verification and Validation (TEVV) Investment Strategy 2015-2018," Assistant Secretary of Defense / Research and Engineering (ASD/R&E), Autonomy Community of Interest (COI), June 2015: http://www.defenseinnovationmarketplace.mil/resources/OSD_ATEVV_STRAT_DIST_A_SIGNED.pdf.

investigated research into changing the current T&E processes and methods for autonomous systems. Finally, AFRL led an OSD-funded seedling effort to investigate licensure-based certification of autonomy. This study is investigating a separate TEVV model for autonomous agents, which is similar to a licensure model for human operators, and how an autonomous agent might be designed to accommodate such an approach. Software design is a major consideration for these software-intensive activities and systems.

- **NASA**: Architecture for SensorWeb for Earth sciences; integrated vehicle health management tools and techniques to enable automated detection, diagnosis, prognosis, and mitigation of adverse events during flight; integrated aircraft control design tools and techniques; and physics-based Multidisciplinary Analysis Optimization (MDAO) framework for cost-effective advanced modeling in development of next-generation aircraft and spacecraft.

- **NIST**: Standards development and testing tools supporting interoperability such as schema validation, semantics, automated test generation (conformance testing), naming and design rules; product data models and modeling tools; methods to facilitate 3-D shape search; research formal methods for software specification; identify sources of performance variance; develop measurement science that accelerates adoption of roots of trust; develop best practices for managing supply chain risk; identify metrics and methodologies for designed-in security; precisely and accurately define classes of software weaknesses to serve as a basis for tool interoperability and proofs that a tool or technique precludes certain classes of weaknesses; run the Static Analysis Tool Exposition (SATE) to understand the contribution of such tools to assurance; convene Software Testing Metrics and Standards workshop to document state of the art in testing and to map gaps and needed research; tools and metrics to support better quality software and software testing and to support innovation in software-dependent industries.

- **NOAA**: Standard and consistent software development practices for environmental modeling; continue adoption of ESMF as part of overall modeling activities; and computer science aspects of software development, including collaboration with universities on programming model for fine-grain parallel architectures.

- **NSF**: Advance core research on the science and engineering of software development and evolution, including formal mathematical/logical foundations and automated development methods, programming languages and methodologies, software testing and analysis, empirical software research, and human-centered computing; coordinate SDP-related areas (e.g., productivity, cost, responsiveness of software, and evolution) in crosscutting topics and programs, including SI^2, SaTC, and effective software design for real-world systems in healthcare, manufacturing, etc.

- **ONR**: Automated generation of secure and robust codes from high-level description (design-entry) of functions that lead to software that is both readable and efficient; to methods that automatically capture and use work flow, thought/design-decision documentation during development and sustainment and leads to implementations that meet performance and security requirements; to technologies for real-time control of distributed and embedded systems; to methods for intelligent orchestration of Web services; to language and system for building secure, federated, distributed information systems; to analysis tools for modeling, testing software component interactions; to software for quantum processing; to automated software de-bloating and de-layering to reduce software complexity, size/attack-surface, and achieve highly efficient, compact, secure programs; and to develop novel architectures and protocols for real-time control of embedded sensors, new reference architectures for embedded systems, and promote reusability.

- **OSD**: The OSD program addresses composability and timing at all scales, computing for real-time and embedded systems, multicore programming, formal methods, computing at the tactical edge, and software architectures. The OSD program is building on prior initiatives such as the Software Producibility Initiative to mature tools and techniques that improve the efficiency of software production for the DoD. Promising techniques include correct-by-construction methods, model-driven development, validation and verification of complex systems (greater than 20 million lines of code), static and dynamic analysis, deterministic behavior in software, interoperable multi-scale and multi-domain models, and efficient execution of distributed and multicore processing.

NITRD Program Coordination

Agencies coordinate their NITRD research activities and plans by PCAs or program focus areas. For each PCA, agency representatives meet in an Interagency Working Group (IWG) or a Coordinating Group (CG) to exchange information and collaborate on research plans and activities such as testbeds, workshops, and cooperative solicitations.[15] Such activities enable agencies to coordinate and focus their R&D resources on important, shared problems with the common goals of making new discoveries and/or developing new technological solutions. For example, IT testbeds provide structured environments, akin to laboratory workbenches, where researchers test hypotheses, perform measurements, and collaborate under conditions similar to real-world environments. For agencies, the economic and engineering benefits of sharing IT testbed environments can be substantial, including avoiding the expense of duplicate facilities. Additional benefits accrue from cultivating a vibrant scientific and intellectual enterprise in which researchers across various agencies, disciplines, and sectors share ideas and results, speeding the overall pace of innovation.

The IWGs[16] are:

- Cybersecurity and Information Assurance (CSIA)

- High End Computing (HEC)

The CGs are:

- High Confidence Software and Systems (HCSS)

- Human Computer Interaction and Information Management (HCI&IM)

- Large Scale Networking (LSN)

- Social, Economic, and Workforce Implications of IT and IT Workforce Development (SEW)

- Software Design and Productivity (SDP)

- Video and Image Analytics (VIA)

The NITRD coordinating structure also includes Senior Steering Groups (SSGs) to focus on emerging science and technology priorities. The SSGs enable senior-level individuals who have the authority to affect or shape the R&D directions of their organizations to collaborate on developing effective R&D strategies for national-level IT challenges. The SSGs are:

- Big Data (BD)

- Cyber Physical Systems (CPS)

- Cybersecurity and Information Assurance Research and Development (CSIA R&D)

- Wireless Spectrum Research and Development (WSRD)

The NITRD Program also supports Communities of Practice (CoPs) that function as forums to enhance R&D collaboration and promote the adoption of advanced IT capabilities developed by government-sponsored IT research. The CoPs are:

- Faster Administration of Science and Technology Education and Research (FASTER)

- Health Information Technology Research and Development (HITRD)

---

[15] The naming of a NITRD group as an Interagency Working Group or a Coordinating Group is historical. There is no functional difference between them today.

[16] A new NITRD group (to be named) is being established to support interagency coordination of R&D activities in robotics and intelligent systems.

Overall NITRD Program coordination is carried out by the Subcommittee on Networking and Information Technology Research and Development, under the aegis of the Committee on Technology (CoT) of the National Science and Technology Council (NSTC). The NITRD Subcommittee convenes three times a year and the IWGs, CGs, SSGs, and CoPs each meet approximately 12 times annually. The NITRD National Coordination Office (NITRD/NCO) provides technical, administrative, and logistical support for the activities of the NITRD Program, including publication of the annual NITRD Supplement to the President's Budget.

For further information about the NITRD Program, please see the NITRD website: www.nitrd.gov.

Additional Program Focus Areas

Big Data (BD)

Participating Agencies: DARPA, DHS, DOE/NNSA, DOE/SC, EPA, NARA, NASA, NIH, NIST, NOAA, NSA, NSF, OSD, USAID, and USGS

The Big Data Senior Steering Group (BD SSG) was formed in early 2011 to identify big data research and development activities across the Federal Government; offer opportunities for coordination among agencies, academia, and the private sector; and help establish the goals for a National Big Data R&D Initiative. Over this period, many agencies established big data programs and initiatives. The BD SSG focus over this past year has been to develop a cross-agency Federal Big Data R&D Strategic Plan. This Plan is expected to be released in early 2016.

Additionally, following a recommendation of the PCAST, the NITRD Subcommittee established the LSDMA PCA as one of the new PCAs under the NITRD Program for the FY 2017 budget reporting cycle. The LSDMA PCA merges the big data R&D areas previously coordinated by the BD SSG and the information management aspects of the HCI&IM PCA previously coordinated by the HCI&IM CG.

Cyber Physical Systems (CPS)

Participating Agencies: AFRL, DHS, DoD Service Research Organizations, DOE, DOT, FAA, FDA, NASA, NIH, NIST, NSA, NSF, OSD, and USDA/NIFA

The Cyber Physical Systems Senior Steering Group (CPS SSG) was established in 2012 in response to an ongoing effort by NITRD agencies to foster a multidisciplinary research agenda to develop the next-generation of engineered systems—systems that depend on ubiquitous cyber control and require very high levels of system assurance. Establishing the CPS SSG also responded to a PCAST recommendation to NITRD to coordinate a focused research effort on NIT-enabled interaction with the physical world.

Cyber-physical systems are smart networked systems with embedded sensors, processors, and actuators that are designed to sense and interact with the physical world (including human users), and support real-time, guaranteed performance in safety-critical applications. In CPS systems, the joint behavior of the "cyber" and "physical" elements of the system is critical—computing, control, sensing, and networking are deeply integrated into every component, and the actions of components and systems must be carefully orchestrated.

Communities across the Nation are examining the potential of advanced technologies to benefit residents, promote economic growth, and create environments that are safer, and more sustainable and workable. The CPS SSG is taking a leadership role in formulating a multiagency R&D strategy for CPS and Internet of Things (IoT) concepts that will give rise to smart and connected communities.

The CPS SSG is also exploring the intersection between CPS and robotics in areas where sharing ideas and coordinating efforts could benefit both fields. This past year, agencies concluded sharing their respective R&D strategies in CPS and robotics, and the CPS SSG convened in September 2015 a community visioning workshop to identify opportunities at the interstices of CPS and robotics R&D. The research is central to building controls, emergency response, energy, healthcare, manufacturing, society, and transportation priority areas, and to cybersecurity, interoperability, privacy, safety, and sociotechnical systems strategic challenges.

Cybersecurity and Information Assurance R&D (CSIA R&D)

Participating Agencies: DARPA, DHS, NIST, NSA, NSF, ODNI, and OSD

The Cybersecurity and Information Assurance R&D Senior Steering Group (CSIA R&D SSG) was formed in response to the 2008 Comprehensive National Cybersecurity Initiative (CNCI) – National Security Presidential Directive 54/Homeland Security Presidential Directive 23. The purpose of the CSIA R&D SSG is to provide overall leadership for cybersecurity R&D coordination, and to streamline decision-making processes to support evolving research and budget priorities. The CSIA R&D SSG is composed of senior representatives of agencies with national cybersecurity leadership positions. The CSIA R&D SSG activities include: leading the implementation of the Federal Cybersecurity R&D Strategic Plan required by the Cybersecurity Enhancement Act of 2014;[17] promoting effective Federal cybersecurity R&D coordination among government agencies and with academia and industry; improving synergy between classified and unclassified Federal research; developing focused activities to help accelerate the transition of research into practice; and examining opportunities to coordinate and strengthen research activities supporting privacy in cyberspace.

Faster Administration of Science and Technology Education and Research (FASTER)

Participating Agencies: AFRL, DOE/SC, DHS, FDIC, IARPA, NARA, NIH, NIST, NOAA, Treasury, and VA

The Federal CIO Council, under the leadership of OMB, coordinates the use of IT systems by Federal agencies. NITRD, under the leadership of OSTP, coordinates federally supported IT research. The FASTER Community of Practice (CoP) is an association of science agency CIOs and/or their advanced technology specialists, organized under NITRD to improve the communication and coordination between the two interagency entities. The primary focus of FASTER is on the IT challenges specific to supporting the Federal scientific research enterprise. Through coordination and collaboration, FASTER seeks to share information on protocols, standards, best practices, technology assessments, and testbeds, and to accelerate the deployment of promising technologies from research into operations.

Health Information Technology R&D (HITRD)

Participating Agencies: AHRQ, CDC, DoD, FDA, NIH, NIST, NSF, ONC, and VA

The Health Information Technology R&D (HITRD) Group was established in 2010 in response to the American Recovery and Reinvestment Act of 2009 (ARRA, P.L. 111-5), which directed the NITRD Program to include Federal R&D programs related to health IT. HITRD provides a forum for sharing information about Federal health IT R&D programs, coordinating health IT R&D plans and activities, and promoting synergies across Federal health IT investments. HITRD's focus is to advance information technology research for improving health. HITRD works collaboratively to articulate health IT R&D needs to policy and decision-makers; pursue interagency opportunities that advance IT research, data sharing, integration and connectivity, and innovative health IT systems; and promote workforce development through building and sustaining a community of health IT researchers to address current and future needs. HITRD is in the early stages of developing a strategic R&D framework to identify opportunities and challenges in health IT research.

---

[17] *Federal Cybersecurity Research and Development Strategic Plan: Ensuring Prosperity and National Security.* February 2016, NSTC: https://www.whitehouse.gov/sites/whitehouse.gov/files/documents/2016_Federal_Cybersecurity_Research_and_Development_Stratgeic_Plan.pdf.

Video and Image Analytics (VIA)

Participating Agencies: DARPA, DHS (CBP, FPS, S&T, TSA), DoD (DODIIS, JIEDDO, NCSC, NGA), DoD Service Research Organizations (AFRL, ARL, NRL), DOI/NPS, DOJ (FBI, NIJ), DOT (FHWA), GSA, NASA, NIH, NIST, NOAA, NSF, ODNI (IARPA, NCTC), and VA

The Video and Image Analytics Coordinating Group (VIA CG) was formed in late 2014 to serve as a vehicle for visible-world video and image analysis technology R&D strategy development, collaboration, and resource-sharing across the Federal Government. The need for video analysis technologies spans the entire Federal Government and many agencies are now engaging in R&D efforts. The VIA CG has provided a forum for agencies to come together to share knowledge, emerging priorities, and resources that they have developed within their R&D efforts. Moreover, the VIA CG is providing a forum for agencies to begin interagency strategic planning and collaboration activities.

Current and planned coordination activities include facilitating interagency collaborations; engaging in strategic discussion on emerging priorities related to video; developing an interagency video analytics R&D strategy; and assessing the external landscape and state-of-the-art through interactions with user communities, industry, academia, the standards community, and the international research community. As part of the strategy development effort, the VIA CG has also launched a standards-focused task group to analyze the very complex standards landscape related to video and video analytics and to identify strategic standards needs. The group is also working with an interagency effort to foster the creation of a cross-cutting community of interest to analyze the needs and opportunities with regard to the growth of video analytics in public safety.

Wireless Spectrum R&D (WSRD)

Participating Agencies: DARPA, DHS, DoD Service Research Organizations, NIJ, FAA, FCC, NASA, NIST, NSA, NSF, NTIA, and OSD

The Wireless Spectrum R&D Senior Steering Group (WSRD SSG) was established in 2010 in response to the June 28, 2010 Presidential Memorandum – Unleashing the Wireless Broadband Revolution. NITRD is supporting the Secretary of Commerce, through NTIA, in consultation with NIST, NSF, DoD, DOJ, NASA, and other agencies, to facilitate research, development, experimentation, and testing by Federal, academic, and private sector researchers and to explore innovative spectrum-sharing technologies. Through a series of workshops and reports, the group has focused on transparency, smart investment, and technology transfer opportunities to develop recommendations that maximize bilateral spectrum sharing between the Federal Government and the private sector.

NITRD Groups and Chairs

Interagency Working Group, Coordinating Group, and Team Chairs

Cyber Security and Information Assurance (CSIA) Interagency Working Group
Co-Chairs
Douglas Maughan, DHS
William D. Newhouse, NIST

High Confidence Software and Systems (HCSS) Coordinating Group
Co-Chairs
David Corman, NSF
William Bradley Martin, NSA
Albert J. Wavering, NIST

High End Computing (HEC) Interagency Working Group
Chair*
Tsengdar Lee, NASA
Co-Chair
Edward Walker, NSF

Human-Computer Interaction and Information Management (HCI&IM) Coordinating Group
Co-Chairs
Sylvia Spengler, NSF
Vacant

Large Scale Networking (LSN) Coordinating Group
Co-Chairs
Robert J. Bonneau, OSD
Vince Dattoria, DOE/SC

LSN Teams:
Joint Engineering Team (JET)
Co-Chairs
Vince Dattoria, DOE/SC
Kevin Thompson, NSF
Middleware and Grid Interagency Coordination (MAGIC) Team
Co-Chairs
Richard Carlson, DOE/SC
Daniel S. Katz, NSF

Social, Economic, and Workforce Implications of IT and IT Workforce Development (SEW) Coordinating Group
Co-Chairs
Arlene de Strulle, NSF
Vacant

SEW Teams:
SEW-Collaboration Team
Co-Chairs
K. Estelle Dodson, NASA
Kara L. Hall, NCI

SEW-Education Team
Co-Chairs
Arlene de Strulle, NSF
William D. Newhouse, NIST (Acting)

Social Computing Team
Co-Chairs
Rebecca Goolsby, ONR
Vacant

Software Design and Productivity (SDP) Coordinating Group
Co-Chairs
Sol Greenspan, NSF
James Kirby, NRL
Ram D. Sriram, NIST

Video and Image Analytics (VIA) Coordinating Group
Chair
John Garofolo, NIST
Co-Chairs
Richard W. Vorder Bruegge, FBI
Patricia Wolfhope, DHS

Senior Steering Group and Community of Practice Chairs
Big Data (BD) Senior Steering Group
Co-Chairs
Chaitanya Baru, NSF
Allen Dearry, NIH

Cyber Physical Systems (CPS) Senior Steering Group
Co-Chairs
Chris L. Greer, NIST
Keith Marzullo, NCO

Cybersecurity and Information Assurance R&D (CSIA R&D) Senior Steering Group
Co-Chairs
Keith Marzullo, NCO
Vacant

Faster Administration of Science and Technology Education and Research (FASTER) Community of Practice (CoP)
Co-Chairs
Robert B. Bohn, NIST
Robert Chadduck, NSF

Health Information Technology R&D (HITRD) Community of Practice (CoP)
Co-Chairs
Wendy J. Nilsen, NSF
Vacant

Wireless Spectrum R&D (WSRD) Senior Steering Group
Co-Chairs
Thyagarajan Nandagopal, NSF
Rangam Subramanian, NTIA

*Darren Smith, formerly with NOAA, was Chair of the HEC IWG through mid-January 2016.

Abbreviations and Acronyms

ACS – Autonomic Cyber Systems

AEH – Airborne electronic hardware

AFOSR – Air Force Office of Scientific Research

AFRL – Air Force Research Laboratory

AHRQ – HHS's Agency for Healthcare Research and Quality

ALCF – Argonne Leadership Computing Facility

ANI – Advanced Networking Initiative

ANL – DOE's Argonne National Laboratory

ARL – Army Research Laboratory

ARO – Army Research Office

ARPA-E – DOE's Advanced Research Projects Agency - Energy

ARSC – Arctic Region Supercomputing Center

ASC – DOE/NNSA's Advanced Simulation and Computing program

ASCR – DOE/SC's Advanced Scientific Computing Research

ASTAM – DHS's Application Security Threat Attack Modeling program

ATC – Air traffic control

ATP – App Testing Portal

BD – Big Data, one of NITRD's Senior Steering Groups

BD2K – NIH's Big Data to Knowledge program

BGPSEC – Border Gateway Protocol Security

BIRN – NIH's Biomedical Informatics Research Network

BISTI – NIH's Biomedical Information Science and Technology Initiative

BlueGene-Q – Latest-generation BlueGene architecture

BLS – U.S. Bureau of Labor Statistics

C3E – ODNI's Computational Cybersecurity in Compromised Environments workshops

C3I – Communications, Command, Control, and Intelligence

CBIIT – NIH's Center for Biomedical Informatics and Information Technology

CCF – Computing and Communication Foundations

CC*DNI – NSF's Campus Cyberinfrastructure – Data, Networking, and Innovation program

CDC – Centers for Disease Control and Prevention

CDS&E – NSF's Computational and Data-Enabled Science and Engineering program

CEDS – DOE/OE's Cybersecurity for Energy Delivery Systems program

CEMMSS – Cyber-enabled Materials, Manufacturing, and Smart Systems

CERDEC – U.S. Army's Communications-Electronics Research, Development, and Engineering Center

CG – Coordinating Group

CIF21 – NSF's Cyberinfrastructure Framework for 21st Century Science and Engineering program

CIO – Chief Information Officer

CISE – NSF's Computer and Information Science and Engineering directorate

CI TraCS – NSF's Fellowships for Transformative Computational Science using CyberInfrastructure

CMATH – DoD/AFRL's Cyber-Based Mission Assurance on Trust-Enhanced Hardware program

CMS – HHS's Centers for Medicare and Medicaid Services

CNCI – Comprehensive National Cybersecurity Initiative

COMPETES – Creating Opportunities to Meaningfully Promote Excellence in Technology, Education, and Science

COOL – DHS's Cybersecurity Organizational/Operational Learning program

CoP – Community of Practice

COTs – Commercial off-the-shelf technologies

CPS – Cyber-physical systems

CRCNS – Collaborative Research in Computational Neuroscience

CSIA – Cybersecurity and Information Assurance, one of NITRD's Program Component Areas

D4SDA – NSF's Data for Scientific Discovery and Action program

DARPA – Defense Advanced Research Projects Agency

DC DWDM – Dispersion compensation dense wavelength division multiplexing

DDDAS – Dynamic Data Driven Applications Systems Program, a joint program of AFOSR and NSF

DDoS – Distributed Denial of Service

DECIDE – Distributed Environment for Critical Infrastructure Decision-making Exercises

DEFT – DARPA's Deep Extraction from Text program

DETER – NSF- and DHS-initiated cyber Defense Technology Experimental Research testbed

DHS – Department of Homeland Security

DIBBs – NSF's Data Infrastructure Building Blocks program, now incorporated into the CC*DNI program

DIMRC – NIH's Disaster Information Management Research Center

DISA – Defense Information Systems Agency

DMZ – Demilitarized Zone; network architecture in which a security layer sits between a trusted, internal network and an untrusted, external network to protect access to the internal network

DNSSEC – Domain Name System Security Extensions

DOC – Department of Commerce

DoD – Department of Defense

DoD (HPCMP) – DoD's High Performance Computing Modernization Program

DoD/TATRC – DoD's Telemedicine and Advanced Technology Research Center

DOE – Department of Energy

DOE/EM – DOE's Office of Environmental Management

DOE/NNSA – DOE's National Nuclear Security Administration

DOE/Oak Ridge – DOE's Oak Ridge National Laboratory

DOE/OE – DOE's Office of Electricity Delivery and Energy Reliability

DOE/SC – DOE's Office of Science

DOJ – Department of Justice

DOT – Department of Transportation

DPIF – Digital Preservation Interoperability Framework International Standard

DREN – DoD's Defense Research and Engineering Network

DTCN – DoD's (ONR) Dynamic Tactical Communications Networks

DTN – Delay-Tolerant Networking

E2E – End-to-End

EARS – Enhancing Access to the Radio Spectrum program

ECI – Exascale Computing Initiative

ED – Department of Education

EHRs – Electronic health records

ENG – NSF's Engineering directorate

EPA – Environmental Protection Agency

ESG – Earth Systems Grid

ESMF – Earth System Modeling Framework

ESnet – DOE's Energy Sciences Network

ESSC – DOE/SC's Energy Sciences network (ESnet) Steering Committee

EUMETSAT – European Organisation for the Exploitation of Meteorological Satellites

FAA – Federal Aviation Administration

FASTER – NITRD's Faster Administration of Science and Technology Education and Research Community of Practice

FBI – Federal Bureau of Investigation

FCC – Federal Communications Commission

FDA – Food and Drug Administration

FHWA – Federal Highway Administration

FIA-NP – NSF's Future Internet Architectures – Next Phase program

FY – Fiscal Year

Gb – Gigabit

GENI – NSF's Global Environment for Networking Innovations program

GIS – Geographic Information System

GOES-R – Geostationary Operational Environmental Satellite R-Series program

GSA – General Services Administration

HCI&IM – Human-Computer Interaction and Information Management, one of NITRD's Program Component Areas

HCSS – High Confidence Software and Systems, one of NITRD's Program Component Areas

HEC – High End Computing

HEC I&A – HEC Infrastructure and Applications, one of NITRD's former Program Component Areas

HEC R&D – HEC Research and Development, one of NITRD's former Program Component Areas

HHS – Department of Health and Human Services

HITRD – NITRD's Health Information Technology Research and Development Community of Practice

HPC – High-performance computing

HPCMP – DoD's High Performance Computing Modernization Program

I/O – Input/output

IARPA – Intelligence Advanced Research Projects Activity

IATS – FHWA'S Integrated Active Transportation System

ICS – Industrial Control Systems

IETF – Internet Engineering Task Force

IHS – Indian Health Services

INCITE – DOE/SC's Innovative and Novel Computational Impact on Theory and Experiment program

InfiniBand – A switched fabric communications link used in high-performance computing and enterprise data centers

INFEWS – NSF's Innovations at the Nexus of Food, Energy, and Water Systems program

Interior – Department of Interior

Internet2 – Higher-education consortium for advanced networking and applications deployment in academic institutions

IPv6 – Internet Protocol, version 6

IRNC – NSF's International Research Network Connections program

ISAP – Multiagency Information Security Automation Program

ISO – International Standards Organization

ISR – Intelligence, Surveillance, and Reconnaissance

IT – Information technology

ITS – Institute of Telecommunications Science

ITSEF – Information Technology Security Entrepreneurs' Forum

IWG – Interagency Working Group

JET – LSN's Joint Engineering Team

JETnets – Federal research networks supporting networking researchers and advanced applications development

JPSS – Joint Polar Satellite System

K-12 – Kindergarten through 12th grade

LANL – DOE's Los Alamos National Laboratory

LBNL – DOE's Lawrence Berkeley National Laboratory
LCF – DOE's Leadership Computing Facility
LLNL – DOE's Lawrence-Livermore National Laboratory
LSN – Large Scale Networking, one of NITRD's Program Component Areas
LTE – Long Term Evolution, a standard for wireless data communications technology
MAGIC – LSN's Middleware and Grid Interagency Coordination Team
MIC – Many integrated cores
MDAO – Multidisciplinary analysis optimization
MGI – Materials Genome Initiative
MOU – Memorandum of Understanding
MURI – Multidisciplinary University Research Initiative
MUSE – DARPA's Mining and Understanding Software Enclaves program
NACS – NASA Advanced Computing Services
NARA – National Archives and Records Administration
NAS – NASA Advanced Supercomputing facility
NASA – National Aeronautics and Space Administration
NCAR – NSF-supported National Center for Atmospheric Research
NCBC – NIH's National Centers for Biomedical Computing
NCCoE – National Cybersecurity Center of Excellence
NCCS – NASA Center for Climate Simulation
NCI – NIH's National Cancer Institute
NCO – NITRD's National Coordination Office
NCR – National Cyber Range program
NERC-CIP – North American Electric Reliability Corporation's Critical Infrastructure Protection
NERSC – DOE/SC's National Energy Research Scientific Computing Center
NeTS – NSF's Networking Technology and Systems program
NextGen – Next Generation Air Transportation System
NEX – NASA Earth Exchange
NFV – Network Functions Virtualization
NGA – National Geospatial-Intelligence Agency
NICE – National Initiative for Cybersecurity Education
NIGMS – NIH's National Institute of General Medical Sciences
NIH – National Institutes of Health
NIJ – DOJ's National Institute of Justice
NIST – National Institute of Standards and Technology
NITRD – Networking and Information Technology Research and Development
NLM – NIH's National Library of Medicine
NOAA – National Oceanic and Atmospheric Administration
NRC – Nuclear Regulatory Commission
NREIP – Naval Research Enterprise Summer Intern Program
NRI – National Robotics Initiative
NRL – Naval Research Laboratory
NSA – National Security Agency
NSCI – National Strategic Computing Initiative
NSF – National Science Foundation
NSF/MPS – NSF's Directorate for Mathematical and Physical Sciences
NSF/SBE – NSF's Directorate for Social, Behavioral, and Economic Sciences
NSTC – National Science and Technology Council
NSTIC – National Strategy for Trusted Identities in Cyberspace

NTIA – National Telecommunications and Information Administration
NTSB – National Transportation Safety Board
NTP – Network Time Protocol
N-Wave – NOAA's high speed network
ODNI – Office of the Director of National Intelligence
OFR – Treasury's Office of Financial Research
OLCF – Oak Ridge Leadership Computing Facility
OMB – White House Office of Management and Budget
ONC – HHS's Office of the National Coordinator for Health Information Technology
ONR – Office of Naval Research
OpenFlow – Open protocol for software-defined networks
ORCA – Online Representations and Certifications Application
ORNL – DOE's Oak Ridge National Laboratory
OS – Operating system
OSD – Office of the Secretary of Defense
OSG – Open Science Grid
OSTP – White House Office of Science and Technology Policy
PCA – Program Component Area
PCAST – President's Council of Advisors on Science and Technology
perfSONAR – performance Services-Oriented Network Architecture
PF – Petaflop(s), a thousand teraflops
PI – Principal investigator
PPAML – DARPA's Probabilistic Programming for Advancing Machine Learning program
PREDICT – DHS's Protected Repository for the Defense of Infrastructure Against Cyber Threats
QOS – Quality of Service
R&D – Research and development
RDA – Research Data Alliance
RDT&E – DoD's Research Development Test & Evaluation programs
ROV – Remotely operated vehicle
RPKI – Resource Public Key Infrastructure
RSIG – Remote Sensing Information Gateway
S&CC – NSF's Smart and Connected Communities program
S&T – Science and technology
S4C – Science for Cybersecurity
S5 – Safe and Secure Software and Systems Symposium
SaTC – NSF's Secure and Trustworthy Cyberspace program
SAMATE – Software Assurance Metrics and Tool Evaluation
SATCOM – Satellite communications
SATE – NIST's Static Analysis Tool Exposition
SBIR – Small Business Innovation Research, a Federal grant program
SCADA – Supervisory control and data acquisition
SCAP – Security Content Automation Protocol
SciDAC – DOE/SC's Scientific Discovery through Advanced Computing program
SDMAV – DOE/SC's Scientific Data Management, Analysis and Visualization for Extreme Scale Science program
SDN – Software Defined Network
SDP – Software Design and Productivity, one of NITRD's Program Component Areas
SDSC – San Diego Supercomputer Center
SEI – Software Engineering Institute

SensorWeb – NASA infrastructure of linked ground and space-based instruments to enable autonomous collaborative observation

SEW – Social, Economic, and Workforce Implications of IT and IT Workforce Development, one of NITRD's Program Component Areas

SEW-Ed – SEW's Education Team

SGIP – Smart Grid Interoperability Panel

SI^2 – NSF's Software Infrastructure for Sustained Innovation program

SME – Subject Matter Expert

SNL – Sandia National Laboratories

SSG – Senior Steering Group

SSPARC – Shared Spectrum Access for Radar and Communications

STAMP – DHS's Static Tool Analysis Modernization Project

STARSS – Secure, Trustworthy, Assured and Resilient Semiconductors and Systems

State – Department of State

STEM – Science, Technology, Engineering, and Mathematics

SWAMP – DHS's Software Assurance Marketplace

SWAP – Size, Weight, And Power

TACC – Texas Advanced Computing Center

TAS – Technology Auditing Service

TCIPG – DHS- and DOE-supported Trustworthy Cyber Infrastructure Protection for the Power Grid program, with initial funding also from NSF

TeraGrid – NSF terascale computing grid, now succeeded by eXtreme Digital (XD) program

TF – Teraflop(s), a trillion floating-point operations per second

TIC – Trusted Internet Connection

TIES – DoD's Tactical Infrastructure Enterprise Services

TIS – NSF's XD Technology Insertion Service program

Treasury – Department of the Treasury

UAS – Unmanned Aircraft Systems

UAV – Unmanned Aerial Vehicle

UQ – Uncertainty Quantification

USAF – United States Air Force

USAID – United States Agency for International Development

USDA – U.S. Department of Agriculture

USGCB – U.S. Government Configuration Baseline

USGS – U.S. Geological Survey

USHIK – United States Health Information Knowledgebase

USSS – United States Secret Service

UtB – NSF's Understanding the Brain program

V&V – Verification and Validation

VA – Department of Veterans Affairs

VOSS – NSF's Virtual Organizations as Sociotechnical Systems program

VSTTE – Verified software, theories, tools, and experiments

VTC – Video Teleconferencing

VVUQ – Verification and Validation, Uncertainty Quantification

WAIL – NSF's Wisconsin Advanced Internet Laboratory

WAN – Wide Area Network

WSRD – Wireless Spectrum Research and Development, one of NITRD's Senior Steering Groups

XD – NSF's eXtreme Digital program

XSEDE – NSF's Extreme Science and Engineering Discovery Environment

www.ingramcontent.com/pod-product-compliance
Lightning Source LLC
Chambersburg PA
CBHW060456060326
40689CB00020B/4554